国家汉办/孔子学院总部
Hanban/Confucius Institute Headquarters

Confucius

Collection of Critical Biographies of Chinese Thinkers

(Concise Edition, Chinese-English)

Editors-in-chief: Zhou Xian, Cheng Aimin

Author: Zhou Qun
Translator: David B. Honey
Expert: Zhang Jing

Nanjing University Press

《中国思想家评传》简明读本 – 中英文版 –

主 编 周 宪 程爱民

国家汉办/孔子学院总部
Hanban/Confucius Institute Headquarters

孔 子

著 者／周 群
译 者／David B. Honey
审 读／张 静

南京大学出版社

Editor: Li Haixia
Cover designed by Zhao Qin

First published 2010
by Nanjing University Press
No. 22, Hankou Road, Nanjing City, 210093
www.NjupCo.com

©2010 Nanjing University Press

Chinese Library Cataloguing in Publication Data
The CIP data for this title is on file with the Chinese Library.

ISBN10: 7-305-06611-5(pbk)
ISBN13: 978-7-305-06611-5(pbk)

《中国思想家评传》简明读本（中英文版）

编 委 会

主 任　许　琳　张异宾
副主任　马箭飞　周　宪
编　委　（按姓氏笔画为序）

马箭飞　王明生　左　健　许　琳　吕浩雪　张异宾
周　宪　周　群　金鑫荣　胡　豪　夏维中　徐兴无
蒋广学　程爱民

主　编　周　宪　程爱民

Editorial Committee

of

Collection of Critical Biographies of Chinese Thinkers

(Concise Edition, Chinese-English)

Executive Director: Xu Lin, Zhang Yibin

Associate Director: Ma Jianfei, Zhou Xian

Members of Committee: Cheng Aimin, Hu Hao, Jiang Guangxue

Jin Xinrong, Lü Haoxue, Ma Jianfei, Wang Mingsheng

Xia Weizhong, Xu Lin, Xu Xingwu, Zhang Yibin

Zhou Qun, Zhou Xian, Zuo Jian

Editors-in-chief: Zhou Xian, Cheng Aimin

Books available in the collection

Confucius
《孔子》
978-7-305-06611-5

Laozi
《老子》
978-7-305-06607-8

Emperor Qin Shihuang
《秦始皇》
978-7-305-06608-5

Li Bai
《李白》
978-7-305-06609-2

Cao Xueqin
《曹雪芹》
978-7-305-06610-8

Du Fu
《杜甫》
978-7-305-06826-3

Zhuangzi
《庄子》
978-7-305-07177-5

Sima Qian
《司马迁》
978-7-305-07294-9

Mencius
《孟子》
978-7-305-07583-4

Mozi
《墨子》
978-7-305-07970-2

总序

General Preface

China is one of the cradles of world civilization, enjoying over five thousand years of history. It has produced many outstanding figures in the history of ancient thought, and left a rich philosophical heritage for both the Chinese people and the entire humanity. The fruit of these thinkers was to establish unique schools that over the long course of history have been continuously interpreted and developed. Today much of these thoughts are as relevant as ever and of extreme vitality for both China and the rest of the world. For instance, the ideal of " humaneness" and the concept of " harmony" taught by Confucius, the founder of Confucianism, have been venerated without ceasing by contemporary China as well as other Asian nations.

Ancient Chinese dynasties came and went, with each new dynasty producing its own scintillating system of thought. These rare and beautiful flowers of philosophy are grounded in the hundred schools vying for attention in pre-Qin times and the broad yet deep classical scholarship of Han and Tang times and in the simple yet profound occult learning of the Wei and Jin dynasties together with the entirely rational learning of Song and Ming Neo-Confucianism. The fertile soil of religious belief was Buddhism's escape from the emptiness of the sensual world and Daoism's spiritual cultivation in the search for identification with the immortals. The founders of these systems of thought included teachers, scholars, poets, politicians, scientists and monks— they made great contributions to such disparate cultural fields in ancient China as philosophy, politics, military science, economics, law, handicrafts, science and technology, literature, art, and religion. The ancient Chinese venerated them for their wisdom and for following moral paths, and called them sages, worthies, saints, wise men, and great masters, etc. Their words and writings, and sometimes their life experiences, constitute the rich matter of ancient Chinese thought distilled by later generations. The accomplishments of Chinese thought are rich and varied, and permeate such spiritual traditions as the harmony between humans and nature, the unification of thought and action, and the need for calmness during vigorous action, synthesizing the old and innovating something new.

Nanjing University Press has persisted over the last twenty years in publishing the 200-book series, *Collection of Critical Biographies of Chinese Thinkers*, under the general editorship of Professor Kuang Yaming, late honorary president of Nanjing University. This collection is the largest-scale project of research on Chinese thinking and culture undertaken since the beginning of the twentieth century. It selected more than 270 outstanding figures from Chinese history, composed their biographies and criticized their

中国是世界文明的发源地之一，有五千多年的文明史。在中国古代思想史上，涌现出了许许多多杰出的思想家，为中华民族乃至整个人类留下了丰富的思想遗产。这些思想成果独树一帜，在漫长的历史中又不断地被阐释、被发展，很多思想对于今天的中国乃至世界而言，仍然历久弥新，极具生命力。比如，儒家学派创始人孔子"仁"的理念、"和"的思想，不仅在当代中国，在其他亚洲国家也一直备受推崇。

古代中国朝代更迭，每一个朝代都有灿烂夺目的思想文化。百家争鸣的先秦诸子、博大宏深的汉唐经学、简易幽远的魏晋玄学、尽心知性的宋明理学是思想学术的奇葩；佛教的色空禅悦、道教的神仙修养是宗教信仰的沃土；其他如经世济民的政治、经济理想，巧夺天工的科技、工艺之道，风雅传神、丹青不老的文学艺术……都蕴涵着丰富的思想。这些思想的创造者中有教师、学者、诗人、政治家、科学家、僧人……他们在中国古代的哲学、政治、军事、经济、法律、工艺、科技、文学、艺术、宗教等各个文明领域内贡献巨大。古代中国人尊敬那些充满智慧、追求道德的人，称呼他们为圣人、贤人、哲人、智者、大师等。他们的言论、著作或被后人总结出来的经验构成了中国古代思想的重要内容，在丰富多彩中贯穿着天人合一、知行合一、刚健中和等精神传统，表现出综合创新的特色。

南京大学出版社坚持20余年，出版了由南京大学已故名誉校长匡亚明教授主编的《中国思想家评传丛书》，这套丛书共200部，是中国20世纪以来最为宏大的中国传统思想文化研究工程，选出了中国历史上270余位杰出人物，为他们写传记，

intellectual accomplishments; all in all, it is a rigorous and refined academic work. On this foundation, we introduce this series of concise readers, which provides much material in a simple format. It includes the cream of the crop of great figures relatively familiar to foreign readers. We have done our best to use plain but vivid language to narrate their human stories of interest; this will convey the wisdom of their thought and display the cultural magnificence of the Chinese people. In the course of spiritually communing with these representative thinkers from ancient China, readers will certainly be able to apprehend the undying essence of thoughts of the Chinese people.

Finally, we are deeply grateful for the support from Hanban/Confucius Institute Headquarters, and the experts from home and abroad for their joint efforts in writing and translating this series.

Editors
November 2009

评论他们的思想成就，是严肃精深的学术著作。在此基础上推出的这套简明读本，则厚积薄发，精选出国外读者相对较为熟悉的伟大人物，力求用简洁生动的语言，通过讲述有趣的人物故事，传达他们的思想智慧，展示中华民族绚烂多姿的文化。读者在和这些中国古代有代表性的思想家的心灵对话中，一定能领略中华民族思想文化生生不息的精髓。

　　最后，我们衷心感谢国家汉办/孔子学院总部对本项目提供了巨大的支持，感谢所有参与此套丛书撰写和翻译工作的中外专家学者为此套丛书所做的辛勤而卓有成效的工作。

<div align="right">

编者

2009年11月

</div>

目录
Contents

一　早年问学

Chapter Ⅰ　Early Studies

Confucius' name was Qiu, his style was Zhongni ❶. Confucius was from the state of Lu (the southwestern part of modern Shandong Province) during the Spring and Autumn Period. He was the first great educator in Chinese history, the most important thinker, and the founder of Confucianism. Confucius was born in the 22nd year of the reign of Duke Xiang of Lu (551 B.C. according to the Western calendar, on August 27). He died in the 16th year of the reign of Duke Ai of Lu (479 B.C.).

Confucius was a descendant of the royal house of the Yin Dynasty. His father was called Shuliang He (His style was Shuliang, and his name was He). He was a warrior in the state of Lu, very brave, and had achieved merits in battle. During the 10th year of Duke Xiang of Lu (563 B.C.), the state of Jin allied itself with the state of Lu and several other states of the feudal princes to attack Biyang (south of modern Zaozhuang City in Shandong Province). Shuliang He also participated in the attack in the siege of Biyang. After the defenders of Biyang lured the army inside the city, they closed the gates and prepared to slaughter the allied troops. Just at this critical moment, Shuliang He rushed to the front and lifted up the gate; this allowed the allied troops to safely escape. Meng Xianzi, the commander of the allied army, praised him as "having the strength of a tiger." Seven years later, in the battle resisting an incursion of the state of Qi, Shuliang He led a three-hundred man party of crack troops to break the siege of Qi right at the critical juncture. And he escorted the two noble brothers of the Zang clan of Lu to the camp of the reinforcements, and then returned, traveling through successive nights, to help continue the defense, at last forcing the retreat of the forces from Qi. Because he became renowned among the feudal princes due to his bravery, he became the grand officer (mayor) of Zouye. Late in life Shuliang He married Lady Yan (name of Zhengzai); she bore Confucius shortly after the marriage. When Confucius was three, Shuliang He died, so Lady Yan took the young Confucius away from Zouye, and returned to Qufu, the capital of the state of Lu; they lived on Que Lane, in the southwestern part of the city.

Being with his mother in Qufu provided a fine cultural environment for Confucius to be raised. Qufu was the fiefdom of the Duke of Zhou, the son of King Wen. When Boqin, the eldest son of the Duke of Zhou, left for Lu, he brought with him many cultural objects and records; he became famous for how he promoted the ritual system of the Zhou royal house. Qufu became the cultural center, second only to that of the capital of the Zhou Dynasty at Luoyi (modern Luoyang, Henan Province). At this time, when a visitor came to Qufu,

孔子名丘，字仲尼❶，春秋时期鲁国（在今山东省西南部）人，是中国历史上第一位伟大的教育家，最重要的思想家，儒家创始人。孔子生于鲁襄公二十二年（公元前551年，夏历八月二十七日），死于鲁哀公十六年（公元前479年）。

孔子是殷朝王室的后代，父亲叫叔梁纥（hé）（字叔梁，名纥），是鲁国的武士，勇力过人，多有战功。鲁襄公十年（公元前563年），晋国联合鲁国等几个诸侯国进攻偪（bī）阳（今山东省枣庄市南），叔梁纥也参加了这场围攻偪阳的战斗。偪阳守军诱联军入城后，关门要消灭联军，在这危急之时，叔梁纥飞步上前，托起悬门，才使联军得以安然撤退。联军统帅孟献子称赞他"有力如虎"。七年之后，在抗击齐国入侵的战斗中，叔梁纥在齐军压境的危急时刻，率领三百名士兵夜间突围，护送鲁国贵族臧氏兄弟到援军营中，又连夜回去继续固守，最终迫使齐军退却。叔梁纥因勇敢而闻名于诸侯，成为陬邑（zōuyè）大夫。叔梁纥晚年娶颜氏（名征在）为妻，婚后不久生孔子。孔子三岁时，叔梁纥去世，颜氏便带着年幼的孔子离开了陬邑，回到了鲁国的都城曲阜，在城西南一个名叫阙（què）里的地方住下。

孔子随母居于曲阜，这为孔子的成长提供了良好的人文环境。曲阜是周文王的儿子周公封国的都城，周公的长子伯禽到鲁国去时，带了很多文物典籍，并以推行周王朝的礼制而闻名天下，曲阜成了仅次于周王朝京城洛邑（今河南省洛阳市）的文化中心。当时有人访问鲁国，看到丰富的文化典籍，感叹道：

❶ 中国古代的男子在二十岁以后，根据人名的含义另取别名，叫"字"。

❶ In ancient China, after a man reaches twenty years of age, he takes another name based on the meaning of his personal name; this is called a "style."

he saw the richness of the culture and the records and remarked with a sigh, "The rites of Zhou are all in the state of Lu." This type of environment, replete in culture, nurtured Confucius in a fine ritual education since his earliest years. Hence, Confucius' reverence for the rites of Zhou is intimately connected with the humanistic environment of Qufu, the capital of the state of Lu. Additionally, Confucius was born in a hereditary scholar family; at that time, hereditary scholars had to learn the rites. Young Confucius was saturated with them; from early on he imitated adults by taking out the vessels used in the rites and playing at performing some rites. Since a young age Confucius was studious and thoughtful, so naturally he was more willing to accept a traditional education. He and his mother relied on each other. When he was young, he lost his standing as an aristocrat, so he learned to take on many menial tasks. Although Confucius led a poor life while young, his experiences deepened his understanding of worldly affairs.

When Confucius was 17, his mother died of illness brought on by overwork. This doubtlessly was a heavy blow to Confucius. His mother, called Yan Zhengzai, placed great importance on her son's education. After the death of Shuliang He she resolutely moved to Qufu to enable Confucius to receive a fine education. She worked tirelessly teaching Confucius, and after Confucius lost his father's love at a young age, the tenderness of her motherly love touched and nurtured Confucius' spirit. After her death, Confucius lost his temporal and spiritual support, and at an early age was forced to walk on the path of life alone. In his youth Confucius was clever yet sober. This was manifested in the course of burying his mother. After Yan Zhengzai's passing away, Confucius wanted to bury his mother with his father in a double burial, but since Confucius lost his father when he was three, he did not know the location of his father's grave. In order to inquire after his father's grave Confucius left his mother's coffin on the side of a busy intersection in order to attract the attention of someone who might know something. As expected, someone emerged from the crowd of onlookers who had some information. This was the mother of a man called Manfu. She told Confucius that the grave of Shuliang He was on the north face of Fang Hill to the east of Qufu. Thereupon, Confucius was able to bury his mother with his father.

In his youth, Confucius learned much about the meaning of life from his own life experiences. One of these experiences made a profound impression on him. Not long after his mother's passing away, the grand officer in power in the state of Lu, the head of the Jisun clan, held a banquet for the nobility. This was an important opportunity for Confucius to meet members of the upper

"周礼都在鲁国了。"这种浓厚的文化氛围，使孔子从小受到了良好的礼仪文明的熏陶。孔子对于周礼的敬仰便与鲁国国都曲阜的人文环境有关。加上孔子生于士族家庭，当时士族必须学习礼仪，幼年的孔子耳濡（rú）目染，很小就模仿大人将祭祀时存放供品用的俎（zǔ）豆等礼器拿出来，做礼仪的游戏。孔子从小好学多思，自然更易于接受传统的教育。孔子与母亲相依为命，年少之时，失去了贵族的地位，所以学会了做很多粗杂活。幼时的孔子虽然过着清贫的生活，但这样的人生经历也使孔子加深了对世事的了解。

孔子十七岁时，他的母亲因积劳成疾而去世，这无疑对孔子是一个巨大的打击。孔子的母亲叫颜征在，很重视对儿子的教育，她在叔梁纥去世后毅然来到了曲阜，使孔子自幼受到了良好的教育。她辛勤劳作，启教孔子，在孔子幼年失去父爱时，以慈祥的母爱滋润孔子的心灵。她的去世，使孔子完全丧失了生活与精神的依托，被迫较早地走上了独立的人生道路。孔子年幼时就聪明沉着，这在他埋葬母亲的过程中得到了体现。颜征在去世后，孔子要将父母合葬，但由于三岁即丧父，孔子并不知道父亲坟墓的位置，孔子为了打听父亲的墓地，将母亲的棺材停放在过往的路口，以引起知情的行人注意。果然，从驻足围观的人群中走出了一位名叫曼父的人的母亲，她告诉孔子，叔梁纥的墓在曲阜城东的防山北面，于是孔子将父母合葬一起。

少年的孔子从生活中获得了许多人生的道理，其中有一件事对孔子的影响十分深刻。孔子母亲去世后不久，鲁国的执政大夫季孙氏举行一个贵族的宴会，这是孔子结交上层名流的重

crust of society. Confucius' father had been a notable warrior, so Confucius gladly set off to attend the banquet. But the family steward of the Jisun clan, Yang Hu, blocked him at the door. Yang Hu stated, "Those invited to the Ji family feast are all men of position. Who invited you?" This was quite a blow to Confucius. This taught Confucius that one could not depend on the meritorious achievements of one's ancestors; one could only depend on one's own unremitting efforts. At the same time, this also taught Confucius how to handle oneself in the human realm through the so-called "way of advance and withdrawal." Confucius "therefore withdrew." ❶ The concept of "withdrawal" not only refers to Confucius' retreat from the Jisun household, but also implies an outlook on life. From this Confucius developed his respect for and adherence to "ritual."

The successive deaths of his father and mother left a deep impact on the life of young Confucius. On the one hand, he was forced to work at various menial jobs, and to depend on his own labor to support himself. On the other hand, the difficulties of trying to survive in this environment disciplined his will, and he redoubled his effort, striving for improvement. From early on Confucius was devoted to learning; the content of his studies included the "Six Arts," which were part of the universal curriculum. This included ritual, music, archery, charioteering, calligraphy, and mathematics, in other words, ritual etiquette, musical performance, the shooting at a target with arrows, driving a chariot, the writing of calligraphy, and mathematical computations. Confucius was an open-minded student. For instance, the Grand Temple dedicated to the performance of ritual sacrifice to the founder of the state of Lu, the Duke of Zhou Dan, was located inside Qufu. A rich store of cultural artifacts from early times was preserved within. Confucius modestly requested information from those who had knowledge about the rites. Whenever he entered the Grand Temple, he would ask about what he did not understand. It got to the point that somebody expressed the following doubt about him: "Who says that the son of Shuliang He understands ritual? He still has a lot that he does not understand and must ask others about." On the one hand, this shows that he had no regular teacher, and that he was willing to learn in a humble manner; on the other hand, it shows that Confucius was already renowned for his knowledge of the rites. In the same way, Confucius was enthusiastic about learning music. He had already learned to play the *qin* and to appreciate music and musical composition from such famous masters as Master Xiangzi. Later when Confucius went to the state of Qi, he discussed music with the Grand Master of Music. Upon hearing the music called "Shao," he became enraptured in its

要机会。孔子的父亲是一位出名的武士，于是孔子也兴冲冲地前去赴宴，谁知却被季氏的家臣阳虎拦住了。阳虎说："季家宴请的是有地位的人，谁宴请你呢！"这对孔子是一个不小的打击，使孔子明白了人不能靠前辈的功劳，而要靠自己的不懈努力。同时，这也使孔子明白了处世的进退之道，孔子"由是退"❶。所谓"退"，不仅仅是从季府退出，还具有人生态度的内涵，由此孔子产生了对"礼"的敬畏与遵从。

早年父母相继去世，对年轻孔子的生活产生了重要影响。一方面，孔子不得不干各种粗杂活，依靠自己的劳动谋求生存。另一方面，艰难的生存环境也磨炼了孔子的意志，他更加刻苦自励，努力精进。孔子早年十分好学，所学的内容首先是当时普遍必须学的"六艺"，即礼、乐、射、御、书、数，也就是礼仪、奏乐、射箭、驾车、书写、计算。孔子虚心问学，如，曲阜城里有祭祀鲁国始祖周公旦的太庙，其中保存了丰富的历史文物，孔子虚心地向知礼的人求教。他进入太庙，经常问不懂的事，乃至于有人发出这样的疑问："谁说叔梁纥这个儿子懂得礼啊？他还有好多不懂的事需要问别人呢。"这一方面说明了孔子学无常师，虚心好学；另一方面也说明孔子在当时已经以知礼而闻名了。同样，对于音乐，孔子也热心学习，他曾向师襄子等有名的乐师学习弹琴、欣赏乐曲。孔子后来到齐国时，与齐太师谈论音乐，听《韶》乐，陶醉于美妙的旋律之中，乃

❶《史记·孔子世家》。

❶ "The Hereditary House of Confucius," in the *Records of the Grand Historian*.

beautiful melodies; so intoxicated he was that he was unable to tell the flavor of meat for a long period of time. Confucius became more than proficient in such military arts as archery and charioteering. After Confucius became famous, somebody commented that although Confucius was broadly learned, he had no particular speciality. Confucius then addressed his disciples, saying "What should I do? Should I drive a horse cart? Or should I be an archer? I think I should drive a horse cart!" From this we can tell that Confucius was an expert at driving. At the same time, Confucius was an adroit archer. When he shot, crowds gathered around him like an encircling wall. On the foundation of mastery over such technical arts, Confucius proceeded to study the ancient classics such as the *Book of Poetry,* the *Book of Documents,* the *Rites,* the *Book of Music,* the *Book of Changes,* and the *Spring and Autumn Annals*, becoming a scholar who was both erudite and accomplished as well as a master of both civil and military arts.

Around the age of 19, Confucius married Lady Qiguan; in the next year a son was born. Because Confucius' father had been renowned for his military exploits and Confucius was known for his knowledge of the rites, the Duke Zhao of Lu presented Confucius with a carp fish upon the birth of his son. Confucius was extremely grateful for this gracious gift from the head of the state, therefore he named his son Kong Li (surname Kong, name of Carp), with the style of Boyu (Fish from the Duke). This period was perhaps the most arduous time in Confucius' life. He became a minor official, once managing a storehouse and once in charge of pasturing cattle and sheep. Confucius took these so-called "menial tasks" very seriously and performed them in an outstanding manner. He kept very accurate accounts while managing the storehouse, and he managed to preserve the pasturage in a flourishing state while letting the cattle and sheep fatten as he grazed. At the same time, Confucius worked as a supervisor over sacrifices to the ancestors and presided over burial ceremonies. In other words, he was a so-called "Ru." * Although these types of positions were also rather low, Confucius performed them equally conscientiously. He said, "In matters of mourning I dare not slack off " ❶ ; that is to say, in matters concerning mourning ceremonies for the dead, he strove to perform every ritual required. However, while working as a Ru Confucius did not hold to the dead letter of tradition in terms of ritual observances; rather, he strove to place the moral meaning of the ceremony first, and be a "Gentlemanly Ru," rich in moral learning. Therefore, Confucius was the true founder of the Confucianism school.

The capital of Zhou Dynasty, Luoyi, was the most important political and

至好长时间食肉而不知肉香。孔子射箭、驾车等武科也学习得游刃有余。当孔子声名卓著之后，有人议论：孔子虽然博学，但并无特别的专长。孔子就对弟子们说："我干什么呢？赶马车吗？做射击手吗？我还是赶马车吧！"可见，孔子的驾车技术十分精湛（zhàn）。同时孔子也深谙（ān）射箭，孔子射箭时，观看的人拥挤得如墙壁一般。在精通这些技艺的基础上，孔子又进而学习古代经典，即《诗》、《书》、《礼》、《乐》、《易》、《春秋》，成为博识多才、文武兼通的学者。

大约十九岁前后，孔子与亓（qí）官氏结婚，第二年儿子出生。因为孔子的父亲叔梁纥有军功，并且孔子也因知礼而闻名，儿子出生后，鲁昭公赐给一条鲤鱼。受到国君如此恩遇，孔子十分感激，于是给儿子命名孔鲤，字伯鱼。这一时期可能是孔子生活比较艰难的时期，孔子做过管理仓库和管理牛羊放牧的小吏。这些"鄙事"孔子同样做得十分认真出色。他管理仓库把账目算得清清楚楚，他管理牛羊放牧使草木茂盛，牛羊肥壮。同时，孔子还做祭祀祖先、主持丧葬仪式的司仪，也就是"儒"。虽然这是颇为卑贱的职业，但孔子同样做得十分认真，他说："丧事不敢不勉。" ❶ 就是说办理丧事也努力尽礼。但是，孔子以儒为业并不拘守于传统儒者的礼仪形式，而是力求做以道义为先、富有道德学问的"君子儒"，因此，孔子是儒学的真正创立者。

周王朝的都城洛邑是中国当时最重要的政治文化中心，从

❶《论语·子罕》。

❶ "Zihan," *Lunyu.*

* Confucian specialist in the rites.

cultural center of the time. Confucius once traveled from Qufu to Luoyi, which was an important trip for him. At the time, after Nangong Jingshu, the son of Meng Xizi who was an aristocrat from the state of Lu, had become one of Confucius' disciples, he suggested to Duke Zhao of Lu to send Confucius and himself to visit Luoyi. The Duke granted Nangong Jingshu's request, and put a chariot, two horses, and a manservant at their service. So Confucius went to Luoyi, and visited some worthies to seek learning. He not only learned music from Chang Hong, more importantly he visited that outstanding thinker Laozi. Laozi was the Zhou royal archivist in charge of records and cultural relics. Confucius had a high opinion of Laozi. In the "Biography of Laozi and Han Feizi" in the *Records of the Grand Historian*, it records that Confucius stated to someone after meeting Laozi, "I know that birds can fly; I know that fish can swim; I know that animals can run. Those that can run may end up in a net; those that can swim may be caught by a hook; those that can fly can be brought down by an arrow. As for dragons, they can rise through the sky by riding the wind and clouds, so we do not know about them. The Laozi whom I met today resembles a dragon flying in the sky!" From this we may see that Laozi was more senior than Confucius and had broader learning. Confucius asked Laozi various questions; Laozi answered each of them in detail. He also shared with Confucius his philosophy on life. Doubtlessly, Confucius benefited greatly from this trip to Luoyi.

Confucius had no regular teacher, but he was good at discovering the strengths and knowledge of common people. He said, "When three people walk with me, among them is certainly my teacher. I select the good from among them and follow it and I correct what is bad." ❶ The meaning is that when three people walk together, among them is one who is worth emulating. Whatever is good about him I will imitate, but if I discover something bad I will correct it.

Confucius was an assiduous and meticulous learner; he strove for thorough and penetrating understanding. For instance, he once studied the *qin* from Master Xiangzi. For 10 days straight he concentrated on one song. Master Xiangzi said, "You can study something new." But Confucius responded, "I have only learned the melody; I have not yet learned the techniques of performance." After a while, Master Xiangzi said, "You have already learned the techniques, and you can now study a new song." But Confucius answered, "I have not yet grasped how to present the aim and appeal of this song." After another period of time, Master Xiangzi said, "You have now learned how to present the aim and appeal of this song, so you can study something new." But

曲阜到洛邑，是孔子人生道路上的一次重要行动。当时，鲁国贵族孟僖子的儿子南宫敬叔在做了孔子的弟子后，曾向鲁昭公建议派他和孔子一起到洛邑去，鲁昭公答应了南宫敬叔的请求，给他们派了一辆车子，两匹马，一个仆人。孔子到洛邑访贤问学，不但向苌（cháng）弘学习音乐，更重要的是见到了另一位杰出的思想家老子。老子是周王室管理文物的官吏。对于老子，孔子有很高的评价，《史记·老子韩非列传》中记载孔子见到老子之后曾对他人说："鸟，我知道它能飞；鱼，我知道它能游；野兽，我知道它能跑。会跑的可能落入网中，会游的可能被钓上来，会飞的可能被箭打下来。至于龙，它可以乘风云飞上天，我们不知道它。我现在所见到的老子，就像天上飞的龙一样啊！"可见，老子是比孔子学问更为广博的长者。孔子向老子提出疑问，老子一一作了详细解答。老子还对孔子说了一些人生哲理。无疑，此次洛邑之行孔子收获很大。

孔子学无常师，他善于发现常人身上所具有的优点与知识，他说："三人行必有我师焉：择其善者而从之，其不善者而改之。"❶意思是说，三人在一起走路，其中一定有值得我师法的人，我将选择好的学习，发现不好的则改正。

孔子学习十分认真细致，务求透彻深入。如，他曾向师襄子学琴，十天时间一直学一个曲子，师襄子说："可以学新的了。"孔子则说："我学了曲调，演奏的技巧还没有学会。"过了一段时间，师襄子又说："技巧已学好了，可以学新曲了。"孔子则说："我还没有领会曲中的志趣韵味。"过了一段时间，

❶　《论语·述而》。

❶　"Shu'er," *Lunyu.*

Confucius responded, "I still do not know for whom this song was composed." After yet another period of time, Confucius said after intense concentration, "I now know who the composer of this song was. It could only be King Wen who has composed it!" Master Xiangzi hastily scrambled to his feet and bowed to Confucius, saying, "My teacher told me that this was the song ' The Etude of King Wen' that had been composed by King Wen!" ❶ It is precisely because he studied so many things that by the age of 30 or so, Confucius had not only learned the "Six Arts," but also mastered what were to be respectfully called the "Six Classics," that is, the ancient texts of the *Book of Documents*, the *Book of Poetry*, the *Book of Changes*, the *Spring and Autumn Annals*, the *Rites*, and the *Book of Music*. At this time Confucius had also observed and analyzed the contemporary decay of the royal house of Zhou, the decline of the rites and the deterioration of music, the political struggles of the feudal princes, and the condition of society. He therefore gradually formulated his own systematic views and principles regarding the world and human life; this established the intellectual and philosophical foundation of this great thinker.

师襄子说："你已学到了曲中的志趣韵味，可以学新的了。"孔子又说："我还不知道这首曲子为谁所作。"又过了一段时间，孔子经过深思之后说："我知道这首曲子的作者是谁了，不是周文王还有谁能作出这首曲呢？"师襄子连忙站起来作揖说："我的老师正是说这是周文王所作的《文王操》啊。"❶ 正是由于多方学习，在三十岁左右，孔子不仅通晓了"六艺"，而且对于后世被尊称为"六经"的《书》、《诗》、《易》、《春秋》、《礼》、《乐》等古代文献也已融会贯通了。这一时期的孔子还观察分析了当时周室衰微、礼崩乐坏、诸侯纷争的政治、社会形势，对世事、人生逐渐形成了一系列看法与原则，奠定了一位伟大思想家的学术与思想基础。

❶ 见《史记·孔子世家》。

❶ For this episode see "The Hereditary House of Confucius," in the *Records of the Grand Historian*.

孔子小时候接受母亲教育

Little Confucius educated by his mother

二 兴教与入齐

Chapter Ⅱ The Beginning of Education and
Move to Qi

Confucius hoped to participate in the political life of the state, and then achieve his own aims. He stated with confidence, "If someone were to employ me to administrate political affairs, within one year I could probably demonstrate results; within three years I would be successful." ❶ Confucius did participate in various political activities of the state of Lu full of faith in himself, but because of the great gap between Confucius' political ideals and the interests of those in power, the respect the latter held for Confucius could not cover the contradiction between these ideals and reality. At this time of political failure, he was able to promulgate his ideals, knowledge, and values through establishing his own private school. Because of changes that occurred in the circumstances of state-run schools during the late Spring and Autumn Period, each level of society experienced changes; the social level that produced those seeking an education expanded as a result. Concurrent with this, because of a deficit in the number of soldiers, those so-called "men of the wilds" who lived on the borders now became eligible for military service to protect the state. The boundary between urban residents of the state and these folk from the hinterland diminished. These country folk also harbored the ambition for getting an education, but lacked the qualifications to study in official schools that had been established for aristocrats. Therefore, the establishment of private schools became a necessity; Confucius thus became the key figure in the rise of private schools. Confucius ran his school with the principle of "teaching all without distinction of class" ; that is to say, he placed no limitations on whom he would teach. Among his disciples were the son of an aristocrat Meng Yizi, as well as such commoners as the father and son tandem of Yan Lu, and Zeng Dian, Min Ziqian, et al.; also included were sons of "base people" such as Ran Boniu, Ran Qiu, and Zhongong who was as poor as a church mouse, Yan Hui who lived in a dilapidated lane, Zilu, the "man of the wilds," and among others. All that students had to pay for tuition was "bundled meat," that is, a bundle of dried meat. Therefore, Confucius was the true historical personage who started the trend of education for commoners. His main teaching method was the catechism, the promulgation of knowledge through the question and answer format. Confucius opened up new avenues of thinking. His teaching method benefited both teacher and student, and used a flexible format. He had no established curriculum; the content of his teaching changed somewhat according to the evolution of his thinking. In his early period, his teaching focused on the "Six Arts," that is, ritual etiquette, musical performance, archery, chariot driving, calligraphy or learning characters, and mathematics. In his later period, he engaged in many discussions with his

孔子希望参与国家政治，实现自己的主张，他自信地说："假如有人用我主持政务，一年便差不多见成效，三年便会取得成功。"❶孔子曾满怀信心地参与鲁国的政治活动，但是，由于统治者的利益与孔子的政治理想存在着巨大的差异，执政者对于孔子的尊崇并不能掩盖理想与现实的矛盾。孔子在政治失意的同时，通过兴办私学这一途径，传播他的理想、知识和价值观念。由于官府办学的局面在春秋晚期发生了动摇，社会各阶层也随着世道发生了变化，要求接受教育的阶层随之增加。同时，由于兵员缺乏，居于边远地区尚未开化的"野人"也可以当兵卫国，居住在城市中的国人与"野人"的界限消除了，这些"野人"也有受教育的愿望，但并不具备进入为贵族而设的官学学习的资格，因此，私学的兴起便成为必然，孔子就是私学真正兴起的关键人物。孔子办学坚持"有教无类"的原则，也就是对学生没有任何限制，其中既有孟懿子这样的贵族子弟，也有平民出身的颜路父子、曾点、闵子骞（qiān）等，还有"贱人"之子如冉伯牛、冉求，"家无置锥之地"的仲弓，住在破陋的小巷中的颜回，"野人"子路等。学生仅交"束脩"也就是一束干肉作为学费。因此，孔子真正是首开平民教育风气的历史人物。孔子主要以问答的形式传播知识，启发思维。教学相长，形式灵活。孔子教学没有固定的教材，教学的内容也随着孔子思想的变化而略有变化，前期主要以"六艺"也就是礼（礼仪）、乐（音乐）、射（射箭）、御（驾车）、书（识字）、数（计算）为教学内容，后期则多与学生讲论"仁"以及体现

❶ 见《论语·子路》。

❶ See "Zilu," *Lunyu*.

disciples about "humaneness," and the way to embody "humaneness" through "loyalty and reciprocity," etc. Of course, moral education and enlightening minds were the fundamental characteristics of Confucius' teachings. Confucius gained a wide reputation due to his opening of a private school, and was supported in this by the aristocrats of Lu. The nobleman in power Meng Xizi, on his deathbed, sent his sons Meng Yizi and Nangong Jingshu to take Confucius as their master and to study ritual from him. The rise of private schools not only started a new chapter in the history of education in ancient China, but also established a forum to hold lectures through which to promulgate ethics and political ideals to improve public morals. This became the main format used to spread culture by later scholars who rushed to imitate it. The formation and development of schools of thought and academic approaches were intimately connected with these types of lectures. This group of lecturers, then, formed the school of thought called Confucianist, which was originally founded by Confucius, and lecture was an important way to transmit learning.

The political situation in the state of Lu at this time was very chaotic. Conflicts broke out between the Ji clan that was in power and another aristocratic clan, ultimately evolving into a struggle between the ruler of Lu, Duke Zhao, and the Ji clan and its allies. Duke Zhao was unable to destroy the Ji clan, so in the end he fled to the state of Qi. Within the seven years after this happened, the state of Lu had no lord, so state affairs were run by the Ji clan. During this time of rebellion in Lu, Confucius went to Qi in the 25th year of Duke Zhao of Lu (517 B.C.). After his arrival, Confucius first served as the family steward of the aristocrat Gao Zhaozi, and hoped to gain an audience with Duke Jing of Qi through Gao Zhaozi's introduction in order to implement his political aspirations. But the political condition in Qi was similar to that of Lu, and the same phenomenon of autocratic rule by hereditary ministers prevailed. But once Duke Jing of Qi asked Confucius about government, Confucius responded with the thought of "Rulers should be rulers, ministers should be ministers, fathers should be fathers, and sons should be sons." This means that a ruler should act like a ruler, a minister should act like a minister, a father should act like a father, and a son should act like a son. Duke Jing of Qi highly valued Confucius' viewpoint. What Confucius said was his doctrine of "the rectification of names." In other words, rulers and ministers should each fulfill their positions, and protect the moral relationship that should prevail between them as well as the political and social order, that is, the inherent "rituals." The second time Duke Jing of Qi asked about government, Confucius

"仁"的"忠恕"之道等。当然，仁德的教化、思想的启迪是孔子教学的根本特质。兴办私学使孔子赢得了广泛的声誉，并得到了鲁国贵族的高度认同，当权贵族孟僖子临终时让自己的儿子孟懿子和南宫敬叔拜孔子为师，随孔子学礼。私学的兴起，不但开启了中国古代教育史的新篇章，而且，设坛讲学，借此传播伦理、政治理想，达到化民成俗的目的，成为后世士人纷纷效法的文化传播方式。中国古代思想学术流派的形成、发展与讲学活动密切相关，讲学成为孔子所创立的儒家学派传播学术的重要方式。

这一时期的鲁国政局混乱，执政的季氏与另一贵族发生矛盾，最后演变成鲁国君主鲁昭公与季氏集团的斗争，鲁昭公未能灭掉季氏，最后逃往齐国。在此后长达七年的时间内，鲁国没有国君，国政仍由季氏操纵。在鲁国内乱时，孔子在鲁昭公二十五年（公元前517年）来到了齐国。到齐国后，孔子首先做齐国贵族高昭子的家臣，并希望通过高昭子拜见齐景公，以便施展自己的政治抱负。但齐国的政治状况也与鲁国相似，世卿专权的现象同样存在。齐景公曾向孔子问政，孔子以"君君，臣臣，父父，子子"相答，意思是君要像君，臣要像臣，父亲要像父亲，儿子要像儿子。齐景公对孔子的观点十分赞赏。孔子所讲的是其"正名"的思想，就是说君臣当各守其位，维护应有的君臣之道以及政治社会秩序，也就是固有的"礼"。齐景公第二次问政时，孔子提出了"为政的关键在于节约财

indicated that "the key to governing lies in being frugal with wealth and riches." ❶ This was directed towards the extravagant and luxurious lifestyles of the aristocrats of Qi and the straitened circumstances of the commoners. According to the historical records, two-thirds of the wealth of the state was siphoned off by the duke, lords, and aristocrats. Qi was building on a large scale, exhausting large amounts of both human and material resources, and complaints from the people were heard everywhere. Given this background, the principle of being frugal with wealth and riches as Confucius taught Duke Jing of Qi as a political principle was actually a criticism of the ruling clique of the state led by Duke Jing of Qi. The Duke did not rebuke Confucius; instead, he wanted to keep Confucius in the state and employ him in an official position with his own land as his source of income. But ultimately, because of the opposition of the great minister Yan Ying, this plan was never realized. Confucius' words were right on target in hitting the crux of the actual political situation. What is lamentable is that, although Duke Jing of Qi was quite respectful of Confucius, he was really unable to employ him. He finally told Confucius frankly that, "I am old and exhausted, and cannot employ you." At the time, someone in Qi wanted to undermine Confucius. Therefore, after two years in Qi, Confucius hurried back to Lu.

After Duke Ding of Lu took over, power fell into the hands of the Ji clan; but the power behind the Ji clan was Yang Hu, their family steward, so he exercised the real authority. Yang Hu not only completely controlled the Ji clan, but also wielded power throughout Lu. This is the case of "a vassal holding the fate of the state in his hands." In such an immoral state, Confucius was unwilling to wallow in the mire with the corrupt clique in power. Yang Hu wanted to use Confucius to elevate his own position, but Confucius detested what Yang Hu was doing, and was unwilling to meet him. One custom of the time was, when a grand official presented a gift to someone of the *shi* class, if the *shi* was not at home to receive the gift personally, then he had to go to the home of the grand official to offer his thanks. Confucius' rank was that of a *shi*, Yang Hu's rank was that of a grand official, so Yang Hu sent the gift of a steamed pig over to Confucius' home when he knew Confucius was not there, and waited for Confucius to come to visit him to offer thanks. Confucius went to offer his thanks, but had first determined when Yang Hu would not be home. Unfortunately, he ran into Yang Hu on the road. Yang Hu then said, "Let me talk with you. Can somebody who is virtuous and talented, yet stands idly while letting the state fall into confusion, be considered to be humane?" When Confucius did not respond, Yang Hu had to keep talking, "No, he cannot be

富"❶。这同样是针对齐国贵族穷奢极欲、百姓困顿的现象而发的。据史书记载，当时齐国民众创造的财富三分之二被公侯贵族掠去。齐国连续大兴土木，耗费了大量的人力物力，民众怨声载道。在这样的背景之下，孔子向齐景公提出节约财富的为政原则，其实就是对齐景公为首的统治集团的批评，但齐景公并没有责怪孔子，反而准备留他在齐国任职，并封田给孔子，最终因为大夫晏婴的反对而未实现。孔子所言，都能切中现实政治的要害，可惜的是齐景公虽然对孔子比较敬重，但并不能真正任用孔子，最后他坦率地对孔子说："我老了，已精力不济，不能任用你了。"当时齐国还有人想加害孔子，于是孔子在齐国度过两年后，又匆匆回到了鲁国。

鲁定公即位之后，大权却掌握在季氏手里，而季氏的权又掌握在家臣阳虎的手里，阳虎不但完全控制了季氏，而且操纵了鲁国的大权，这就是所谓的"陪臣执国命"。孔子身处这无道的乱邦，决不肯与这些胡作非为的执政者同流合污。阳虎想借孔子抬高自己的地位，但孔子深恶阳虎的所作所为，不愿与他相见。当时有这样的习俗：大夫赠送礼物给士，如果士不在家当面接受，便要到大夫家拜谢。孔子的爵位是士，阳虎的爵位是大夫，阳虎便乘孔子不在家时将一只蒸熟的小猪送给孔子，等着孔子回来拜谢。而孔子则打听到阳虎不在家时前去道谢，不巧在途中相遇，阳虎说："来，我跟你说：有德有才而听任国事迷茫，这能算是仁者吗？"孔子不回答，阳虎只得自己说："不算啊。很想从政而又屡失时机，能算是

❶ 见《史记·孔子世家》。

❶ See "The Hereditary House of Confucius," in the *Records of the Grand Historian*.

considered humane. Can somebody who wishes to participate in government, yet does not take advantage of the opportunity, be considered wise?" Since Confucius again did not respond, Yang Hu again kept talking, "No, he cannot. Time passes very quickly, and it will not wait for you." Confucius had answered none of Yang Hu's questions, but now he said one sentence, "I had planned to participate in government." ❶ These are the words that Confucius should say as part of the customary way to respond. While Yang Hu was in power and the state of Lu was in such a chaotic condition, Confucius did never serve in office. Instead, he concentrated his energies on mastering the *Book of Poetry*, the *Book of Documents*, the *Rites*, and the *Book of Music*, while accepting disciples from all over and engaging in the educational activities that he loved so well. During this period, the fame of Confucius in accepting disciples and lecturing spread near and far. According to one record, "His disciples increased, and some came from distant places; all of them studied under Confucius." ❷

智者吗？"孔子仍不作答，阳虎只得说："不算啊。岁月过得很快啊，不会等你的。"阳虎几次发问孔子都不回答，最后孔子才说了句："我打算从政的。"❶ 这是孔子礼尚往来的应托之辞，在阳虎为政，鲁国乱象环生之时，孔子并没有做官，而仍然集中精力修习《诗》、《书》、《礼》、《乐》，广收弟子，从事自己所热爱的教育活动。这一时期孔子收徒讲学的活动已声名远播，据记载："弟子更多，有些从远方来，都跟从孔子学习。"❷

❶ 见《论语·阳货》。
❷ 见《史记·孔子世家》。

❶ See "Yang Huo," *Lunyu*.
❷ See "The Hereditary House of Confucius," in the *Records of the Grand Historian*.

春秋晚期青铜器牺尊

Bronze Zun of the late Spring and Autumn Period

三　从政经历

Chapter Ⅲ　Experience in Government

When Confucius turned 51 years old during the ninth year of the reign of Duke Ding of Lu (501 B.C.), a real opportunity presented itself to participate in politics. At this time, the political situation in Lu was changing greatly: Zhong Lianghuai, the family steward of Ji Huanzi, was brought under control, so Yang Hu left the state. During this year, Confucius was appointed as a steward at the capital. Although this position was not very eminent, being equivalent to the county magistrate of modern China, still it was the first time that Confucius served in office. The political results he earned were evident, and he became an example for his colleagues to imitate. Not long after, he was elevated to the office of minister of works. Confucius was good at conducting political affairs by guiding actions according to circumstances; therefore, he achieved some accomplishments in this office. Again, after a short period of time, Confucius was promoted to be the minister of criminal justice. This position was the senior official in charge of the state judicial and penal systems, and also in charge of keeping order in society. Confucius' rank was now that of a grand minister, equal to that of the three great prime ministers over personnel, works, and war. His position was eminent and his authority was great. Confucius served for about three years as the minister of criminal justice.

The minister of criminal justice presided over administering punishment and suits at law. But at the time, there was no detailed legal code governing lawsuits. Therefore, the personal qualities and administrative style of adjudicating cases of the official played important roles in reaching fair and impartial decisions. When Confucius was deciding cases, he was able to seek the views of a broad range of persons before making his decisions. In this way, he largely avoided mistakes in his judgments. This rather democratic style of trying cases was rarely seen at the time. Of course, while in office as minister of criminal justice, Confucius had his successes as well as his failures.

After Confucius had been in office for a short while, the rulers of both Lu and Qi decided to convene a great conference at Jiagu in Qi (within the borders of modern Laiwu County, Shandong Province) to conclude a treaty. But each side had a different purpose in concluding this treaty: Qi hoped to gain the support of Lu in its competition with Jin for hegemony, while Lu wanted to recover some territory that had been seized a few years earlier by Qi. At this time, Confucius served as the master of ceremonies for Lu at the conference. At the conclusion of the exchange of ceremonial gifts between the two rulers of state, the master of ceremonies of Qi first requested a performance of songs from all regions. A group of musicians wielding a variety of weapons noisily

鲁定公九年（公元前501年），孔子五十一岁时，真正从政的机会到了。这时，鲁国的政治局面发生了很大的变化：季桓子的家臣仲梁怀被制服，阳虎出走。这一年孔子被鲁国任命为中都宰，虽然职位不很高，相当于后世的县长，但却是孔子第一次从政，政绩可观，成为同行学习的榜样。不久，又由中都宰升任为司空，孔子为政能因势利导，所以在其任上也颇具成就。不久孔子又由司空升为大司寇。大司寇是掌管国家司法、刑狱和社会治安的最高长官，爵位为大夫，与司徒、司马、司空三卿并列，位高权重。孔子担任司寇约三年左右。

司寇一职主管刑狱，当时并没有详细的诉讼法律条文，因此，能否做到公正明鉴，任职者的个人素质、办案作风往往起到重要的作用。孔子断案时，能够多方听取别人的意见，最后才作出裁决，这样就最大限度地避免了误判，这种颇具民主作风的判案方式在当时十分少见。当然，在大司寇任上，孔子既有成功，也有过失败。

上任不久，齐国和鲁国国君商定在齐国的夹谷（今山东省莱芜县境内）举行大盟会，双方盟会的目的各不相同：齐国期望在与晋国争霸过程中得到鲁国的支持，而鲁国则想要回几年前被齐国强占的土地。孔子在此次盟会中担任鲁国的司仪。当双方国君献酬礼仪结束后，齐国的司仪首先请奏四方之乐，随即一批夹带着各类兵器的乐队吵吵嚷嚷地登场，试图在混乱

took the stage, intending to abduct the ruler of Lu during the distraction of the performance. But Confucius walked up and berated them, saying, "The rulers of our two states are at this conference; how can you then perform the music of barbarians?" He demanded that the musicians withdraw. Duke Jing of Qi felt rather shameful, and acquiesced to Confucius' suggestion. After a while, the Qi master of ceremonies allowed a troupe of dwarfs and clowns to come forward and perform "Palace Music." Confucius once more strode up to the steps of the stage and said, "Those who mock and confuse the ruler should be executed." ❶ He demanded that they withdraw. Again, Duke Jing of Qi had to acquiesce to Confucius' suggestion. Before they signed the treaty, Qi unilaterally added a provision to the effect that when Qi went out on campaign, Lu was required to dispatch three hundred war chariots in support; Confucius added the condition that Qi return the territory of Wenyang to Lu. After Duke Jing of Qi returned home, he was full of admiration for Confucius. He once said to his ministers, "Confucius of Lu aides his lord of state with the way of the gentleman; yet you taught me using the way of the barbarian, making me offend the ruler of Lu. What should we do?" The ministers pointed out that when a gentleman commits an error, he should repay the other side with something concrete. Thereupon Duke Jing of Qi returned the territories of Yun, Wenyang, and Guiyin. Ultimately, the treaty of Jiagu between Lu and Qi worked out to Lu's advantage. Confucius played an important role in this particular case of diplomacy. In order to acknowledge the merit accomplished by Confucius, Lu built a new town in the newly returned territory of Guiyin, and called it "Thanksgiving Town." The treaty of Jiagu greatly increased the fame of Confucius. Duke Ding of Lu and Ji Huanzi, who held actual power, both greatly esteemed Confucius. During the 14th year of Duke Ding (496 B.C.), Confucius "served as acting prime minister in his office of minister of criminal justice" ; that is, he temporarily acted in the highest administrative office, behind only Duke Ding of Lu and Ji Huanzi in rank. Thus he became the Number Three man in the state. During this period, one great thing Confucius accomplished was to have demolished the city walls of the towns occupied by the three aristocratic clans of Jisun, Mengsun, and Shusun. This is what in the historical records is known as "destroying the three capitals." But this experience also made Confucius experience the bitter fruit of complications of real politics.

The royal house of Lu at this time was in a state of decline. The "Three Huans" (the descendents of the three sons of Duke Huan of Lu, who respectively served as the three ministers of state in the offices of minister of

中劫持鲁国国君，孔子上前责问说："我们两国国君在此盟会，怎么演奏野蛮人的音乐？"要求将其撤去。齐景公颇为惭愧，只得听从孔子建议。一会儿，齐国的司仪又让一批侏儒小丑上前演奏所谓"宫中之乐"，孔子又走上台阶说："戏弄惑乱君主的，应被处死。"❶ 要求撤去，齐景公只得听从孔子的建议。在盟约签字之前，齐国单方面加上了齐军出兵需鲁国派三百辆兵车相配合的内容，孔子则提出齐国必须归还汶阳给鲁国为条件。齐景公归国后，对孔子深为叹服，对群臣说："鲁国的孔子以君子之道辅助国君，而你们则以夷狄之道来教我，使我得罪了鲁国君主。你们看怎么办？"群臣提出，君子有过失，应当以实质的东西回报对方，于是齐景公归还了郓、汶阳、龟阴的土地给鲁国。最终，齐鲁两国的夹谷之会以鲁国的胜利而告终。孔子在这次外交活动中起到了重要的作用，鲁国为了表彰孔子的功绩，在齐国归还的龟阴筑城，名叫谢城。夹谷盟会使孔子的声望大增，鲁定公与掌握实权的季桓子对孔子更加倚重。鲁定公十四年（公元前496年），孔子"由大司寇行摄相事"，就是代行鲁国的最高行政职务，地位在鲁定公、季桓子之后，成为鲁国的第三号人物。在这期间，孔子所做的一件大事是拆除季孙氏、孟孙氏、叔孙氏三家贵族盘踞的城堡，也就是史书记载的"堕(毁坏)三都"，但这也使孔子第一次尝到了复杂的现实政治的苦果。

当时的鲁国王室衰微，掌握鲁国实权的是"三桓"（鲁桓公三个儿子的后裔，分别任司空、司马、司徒，为鲁国三卿），

❶ 见《史记·孔子世家》。

❶ See "The Hereditary House of Confucius," in the *Records of the Grand Historian*.

works, minister of war, and minister of personnel) held power in the state, but their family stewards had erected fortresses on the lands belonging to these clans and openly opposed them. The "Three Huans" lived in Qufu, and were sorely pressed by their family stewards but could do nothing about it. For instance, Yang Hu, the family steward of Ji Huanzi, once incarcerated him, and did not release him until he acknowledged his failure. Another family steward of Ji Huanzi, Gongshan Buniu, once made contact with Yang Hu, and attempted to change the official successor of the "Three Huans" to one of Yang Hu's men. In this way the "Three Huans" could be more easily controlled. Therefore, a strange situation was created where the family stewards controlled Ji Huanzi, and Ji Huanzi controlled Duke Ding of Lu. By demolishing the walls of these fortified towns, Confucius would eliminate the strongholds of these family stewards as bases from which to oppose the "Three Huans." On the surface, this move advocated by Confucius would resolve the conflict between the "Three Huans" and their family stewards, and would be beneficial to the "Three Huans." This would suppress their family stewards and make them loyal once again to their masters. But in reality, it would also work to resolve the conflict between the royal house and the "Three Huans," to weaken the latter's power and make them follow the way of loyal servants. This would restore Duke Ding to actual political power; this plan, therefore, was supported by Duke Ding. Confucius first took down the walls of Hou, the headquarters of the Shusun clan. But when demolishing the walls of Fei, the headquarters of the Jisun clan, he encountered the strong opposition of Gongshan Buniu, the family steward of the Ji clan. Gongshan Buniu first gained the upper hand by attacking Qufu; Confucius led the Lu troops in making a counterattack and was victorious. This resulted in Gongshan Buniu fleeing to Qi; the walls of Fei were finally demolished. All that was left was the fortress of the Mengsun clan. The family steward of the Mengsun clan, Gonglian Chufu, had always been loyal to the Mengsun clan, and had never harbored any thoughts of rebellion. This was very different from the situation of the Jisun and Shusun clans. So demolishing the walls of the Mengsun clan's fortress was not beneficial. The family steward therefore advised the head of the Mengsun clan, saying, "We are close to Qi territory; if we demolish the walls, then troops from Qi will enter from our northern gate. Also, this fortress is the safeguard of the Mengsun clan; if we do not have this, then we will not have a Mengsun clan." The head of the Mengsun clan accepted this advice from his family steward. Superficially he did not oppose the destruction of the fortress, but he secretly supported his family steward in opposing the move with all his might.

而"三桓"的家臣们则在"三桓"的封地上大建城堡，对抗"三桓"。"三桓"住在曲阜，深受家臣之害而无能为力。比如，季桓子的家臣阳虎就曾将季桓子囚禁起来，直到季桓子承认失败才将他放出。季桓子的另一家臣公山不狃（niǔ）还曾联合阳虎，试图把"三桓"的继承人换成亲近阳虎的人，以便更好地操纵"三桓"。因此，当时形成了家臣挟制季桓子，季桓子挟制鲁定公的奇怪局面。拆除他们的城堡就可以消除家臣对抗"三桓"的据点。孔子提出的这一主张表面上是解决"三桓"与家臣之间的矛盾，是为了"三桓"的利益，贬抑"三桓"的家臣，使其忠实于主人，但实际上也是为了解决王室与"三桓"之间的矛盾，削弱"三桓"的实力，使其谨守为臣之道，重新确立鲁定公的实际统治权力，因此受到了鲁定公的支持。孔子首先拆掉了叔孙氏的郈都。但在拆毁季孙氏的费都时，却遭到了季氏家臣公山不狃的强烈反对，公山不狃先发制人，进攻曲阜，孔子率领鲁国的军队反击，取得了胜利，追使公山不狃逃奔齐国，终于拆毁了费都。最后剩下了孟孙氏的城堡，孟孙氏的家臣公敛处父一贯忠于孟孙氏，从无叛意，这与季孙氏、叔孙氏的情况有很大不同，拆除城堡对孟孙氏并无益处。家臣建议孟孙氏说："这里靠近齐国，如果拆除城堡，齐国军队就会从北门进来。而且这里是孟孙氏的保障，没有这个城堡就没有孟孙氏。"孟孙氏采纳了家臣的建议，表面上不反对拆毁城

The other clans, the Jisuns and the Shusuns, also silently assented to this perfunctory attitude of the Mengsun clan. So even when Duke Ding of Lu came and personally oversaw the attack, Lu was unable to conquer them.

The failure of this political reform alarmed the "Three Huans" even more; the intimate cooperative relationship between Confucius and the Jisun clan fell apart because of this. Conflicts between Confucius and the aristocracy of the state of Lu came into the open, and the conditions that permitted him to realize his political aims in Lu were lost. It was right at this time that the state of Qi presented to the Lu ruler 80 beautiful singers and dancers and 120 outstanding horses to distract the attention of the Lu ruler and his ministers. As expected, Duke Ding of Lu and Ji Huanzi spent entire days lost in revelry on the music and dancing and neglected political affairs. After Ji Huanzi accepted the lovely women and valuable horses, he did not handle political affairs for three days, and after sacrificing to heaven and earth, did not share the sacrificial meat with his courtiers as required by ritual. Confucius was thoroughly disappointed with those in power in Lu. Therefore, he decided to leave his homeland, the state of Lu; he thus began a period of 14 years of travel throughout various states. It is not hard to imagine Confucius' bitter feelings on leaving his homeland that he loved so deeply. At this time, Confucius was 55 years old.

堡，但暗中却支持家臣全力反抗，季孙氏与叔孙氏也默许了孟孙氏的敷衍态度，即使鲁定公亲自督战也未能攻克。

这次政治改革的失败使"三桓"更加警觉，孔子与季孙氏的亲密合作关系也随之解体，孔子与鲁国贵族之间的矛盾暴露了出来，他失去了在鲁国施展政治抱负的条件。正在这时，齐国为了瓦解鲁国君臣的意志，挑选了能歌善舞的美女八十人、骏马一百二十匹送给鲁国君臣。果然，鲁定公和季桓子等人整日沉溺于歌舞而懈怠了政事。季桓子接受了齐国的美女和宝马后，三日不听政，在祭祀天地之后，又不按礼送祭肉给大夫。孔子对鲁国的当政者彻底失望了，于是，决定离开他的故乡——鲁国，开始十四年之久的周游列国之旅。离开深深眷恋的父母之邦，孔子凄楚的心情不难想见。这一年，孔子五十五岁。

孔子周游列国示意图

The map of Confucius' traveling

四 周游列国

Chapter IV Travel from State to State

During the 14 years between the 13th year of Duke Ding of Lu (497 B.C.) and the 11th year of Duke Ai of Lu (484 B.C.), Confucius traveled throughout such states as Wei, Chen, Cao, Song, Zheng, and Cai; among these states, he stayed the longest in Wei and Chen. Confucius hoped to proclaim his political and moral philosophy in these states, and, under the proper conditions, serve in the government to achieve his ideals.

The first stop in the travels of Confucius and his party was Wei, a state on the western border of Lu. There were many advantages in going to Wei: Among Confucius' disciples were many from Wei, and Confucius had a great reputation in Wei. The virtuous grand official who was good at self-improvement, Qu Boyu, was there; Qu Boyu had once before sent a representative to visit Confucius. And Lu and Wei had both been founded by descendants of the King Wen of Zhou. Finally, Wei had political and cultural backgrounds similar to Lu's; the situation was precisely described as "In politics, Lu and Wei are brothers." ❶ Most importantly, Yan Zhuozou, the elder brother of Confucius' disciple Zilu's wife, was an official in Wei; he was a grand official noted for his virtue. Confucius and his party stayed with Yan Zhuozou when they first came to Wei. After his arrival in Wei, Confucius was greatly esteemed by Duke Ling of Wei because of Confucius' great reputation. The duke granted Confucius an annual income of 60,000 pecks of grain. However, Confucius did not stay in Wei for very long. The reason was, previously Confucius had had some contact with Gongshu Xu, the son of the virtuous grand official Wenzi of Wei. But when Gongshu Xu plotted to get rid of Madam Nanzi, the wife of Duke Ling of Wei, he was discovered and so rebelled. When he failed, he had to flee to Lu. Confucius was afraid of being implicated, so he left the state of Wei.

When Confucius left Wei, he was preparing to travel to the state of Chen. However, on the way when he had reached Kuang (within the borders of Changhuan County in modern Henan Province), he was detained for several days when he was mistaken for Yang Hu, who had previously pillaged the area. Confucius and his party had to return to Wei and stay with the virtuous grand official Qu Boyu. After living in Wei for three or four years, Confucius decided to depart again. The main reason was that Confucius' political ideals on state rule were different from those of Duke Ling of Wei, and Duke Ling's courteous treatment of Confucius was merely intended to utilize Confucius as a figurehead of ritual propriety and of virtue. Not long after Confucius had returned to Wei, he and the duke and their retainers were taking a trip in chariots. The duke and his wife were riding in the front chariot, while

从鲁定公十三年（公元前497年）到鲁哀公十一年（公元前484年）这十四年之间，孔子先后游历了卫、陈、曹、宋、郑、蔡等国，其中，居住时间较长的是卫国和陈国。孔子希望在这些国家宣传自己的政治、道德理念，如有合适的条件也可以通过做官而实现自己的理想。

孔子一行首先到了鲁国西面的近邻卫国。去卫国有许多有利条件：孔子的弟子中有多人是卫国人，孔子在卫国具有很大的影响；卫国有蘧（qú）伯玉那样善于改过的贤大夫，蘧伯玉还曾派人来看望过孔子；鲁、卫都是周文王的后代，卫国有与鲁国相似的政治环境与文化背景，正所谓"鲁卫之政，兄弟也"❶；更重要的是孔子学生子路的妻兄颜浊邹在卫国做官，是一位有名的贤大夫。孔子一行来到了卫国，在颜浊邹家住下。到卫国后，由于孔子当时已具有很高的声望，卫灵公对孔子颇为敬重，给予孔子每年六万斗粮食作为俸禄。但是，孔子这次在卫国的时间并不长，原因是卫国贤大夫文子的儿子公叔戌曾与孔子有交往，但公叔戌想要除掉卫灵公的夫人南子，被发现而准备叛乱不成，逃亡鲁国。孔子怕连累获罪而离开了卫国。

孔子离开卫国后准备到陈国去，在走到匡（今河南长垣县境）这个地方时，被当地人误认为是曾带兵侵扰过匡人的阳虎而被拘数日，孔子一行不得已又回到卫国，住在卫国的贤大夫蘧伯玉的家中。在卫国留居了三四年后，孔子还是决定离开卫国，主要原因是孔子的治国理念与卫灵公不同，卫灵公善待孔子仅是想利用孔子作为礼贤的招牌而已。这次重返卫国后不久，卫灵公与孔子等人乘车出行，卫灵公与夫人坐前面一辆车，让

❶《论语·子路》。

❶ "Zilu," *Lunyu*.

Confucius was in the second chariot. Confucius sighed and said, "I have never seen anyone who loved virtue as much as he loved female beauty." ❶ Duke Ling of Wei's attention was on his troops, and he did not care much for moral rule or humane government. Confucius was very disappointed by this. The *Analects* records the following: Duke Ling of Wei asked Confucius about military formations; Confucius responded, "I have learned something about rites and ceremonies, but I have not learned anything about military matters." The next day, Confucius left Wei. From this we can see that difference in political ideals was an important reason for Confucius leaving Wei. Confucius planned to go to the neighboring state of Jin and visit the commander-in-chief at the headquarters, Zhao Jianzi. But right when Confucius and his party were preparing to cross the Yellow River, they received the message that Zhao Jianzi had killed two virtuous officials who helped him before he had gained power. Confucius was deeply shocked, and sighed as he spoke to the water flowing by, "This boundless extent of the Yellow River is so beautiful, but I cannot cross over it to the west. This perhaps is the decree of fate." ❷ Thereupon, he once again returned to the house of Qu Boyu in Wei. After Duke Ling of Wei died, a struggle broke out between father and son for power; this developed into a chaotic situation, so Confucius had to leave the state again. This time he headed for the state of Chen.

When Confucius and his party were passing by the state of Song on their way to Chen, they heard that Sima Huanzhui was seeking the secret of immortal life. He had ordered a large group of workers to carve a stone coffin that was still not finished after three years. Confucius was deeply grieved by this act of recruiting the masses into forced labor, and so he hoped that Sima Huanzhui would die quickly and lose his immortality. Therefore, Huanzhui toppled down a great tree on the grounds where Confucius and his party practised their ritual ceremonies as a warning to Confucius. His disciples were concerned with Confucius' safety, but Confucius spoke to them calmly, saying, "Heaven granted this virtue to me; what can Huanzhui do to me?" ❸ Confucius believed that the virtuous conduct of a person could affect his fate. Nevertheless, at the urging of his disciples, Confucius left the state of Song as quickly as possible. In order to escape from the pursuit of Huanzhui, they changed their route from the original plan of heading south towards Chen to travel to the west, and went to Chen via the state of Zheng.

The 60-year-old Confucius finally made it to Chen, which he had been trying to visit for a long time; he lived in the house of Sicheng Zhenzi, a grand

孔子坐第二辆车，孔子慨叹道："我没有看到过喜好德行如同喜好美色那样的人啊。"❶卫灵公关注军旅之事而并不关心德治与仁政，对此，孔子深表失望。《论语》中有这样的记载，卫灵公向孔子问军队列阵之法，孔子说："礼仪的事，我曾经听到过；军旅的事，我从来没有学习过。"第二天，孔子便离开了卫国。可见，政治理念有别是孔子离开卫国的重要原因。孔子打算到卫国的邻国晋国去见中军元帅赵简子，正当他们一行准备西渡黄河时，传来了消息：赵简子杀害了在他执政之前帮助过他的两位贤士，孔子深感震惊，对着滔滔黄河水感叹道："浩渺的黄河之水是多么美丽啊，但是我不能西渡黄河了，这也许是命运所决定的吧！"❷于是重新回到了卫国蘧伯玉家。卫灵公死后，卫国发生了父子争夺君位的斗争，陷入混乱局面，孔子不得不又离开卫国，前往陈国。

　　孔子一行前往陈国，路过宋国时，听说宋国的司马桓魋（zhuī）想死后不朽，令大批工匠为他做石椁，三年未成，孔子对桓魋奴役民众的举动非常痛恨，真希望他早死速朽。因此，桓魋便将孔子一行习礼场所的一棵大树弄倒了，以警告孔子。弟子们都为孔子的安全担心，孔子镇定坦然地说："天赋予我这样的品德，桓魋能把我怎样呢？"❸孔子认为德行的修持能关系到人的命运。虽然如此，孔子在弟子们的劝说下还是迅速离开了宋国。为了防备桓魋的追击，他们改变了原定南向陈国的计划，改道西行，经郑国而往陈国。

　　六十岁的孔子来到他向往已久的陈国，住在陈国大夫司城

❶ 见《史记·孔子世家》。
❷ 见《史记·孔子世家》。
❸ 见《论语·述而》。

❶ See "The Hereditary House of Confucius," in the *Records of the Grand Historian*.
❷ See "The Hereditary House of Confucius," in the *Records of the Grand Historian*.
❸ See "Shu'er," *Lunyu*.

official of Chen. The ruler of Chen, Duke Min, wasted no time in summoning Confucius. He greatly esteemed Confucius' erudition and regarded Confucius as an honored guest. However, during the few years spent in Chen, Confucius was unable to achieve his own political aims. In 489 B.C., the state of Wu attacked Chen. King Zhao of Chu personally led a force to aid Chen. But he died of illness in the midst of his army, so the Chu troops were forced to withdraw. The Wu army attacked all the way up to Wanqiu, the capital of Chen. Confucius and his party left Wanqiu in a great hurry. Because of the war between Wu and Chu, and food supplies were scarce, Confucius and his party arrived at the boundary between Chen and Cai with supplies exhausted. Under such straights, his disciples expressed their dissatisfaction and frustration. Despite all of this, Confucius was calm and composed, singing while accompanying himself on the *qin* without stop. His disciples were deeply moved by this, and ultimately were able to make it through this difficulty. When Confucius and his party reached Fuhan (modern Xinyang City, Henan Province), they were warmly received by a grand official of Chu, Shen Zhuliang (also called Duke Ye because of his fiefdom in the land of Ye). Confucius discussed political affairs with him, and proposed an ideal form of government that would cause those in distant lands being willing to come in submission, and those near at home to become even closer and more united. Afterwards, Duke Ye asked Confucius' disciple Zilu what type of person Confucius was. Zilu could not answer. So Confucius said, "You should have told him I am a person who gets too excited to eat, who forgets his sorrow in joy, and who does not realize that old age is approaching." ❶ This is Confucius' own summary of the characteristics of his life, and the best type of education and encouragement for his students. Confucius traveled throughout the state of Chu, and gained a better understanding of the customs, character of the people, history, and culture of Chu.

Confucius traveled for many years, and although he promulgated his philosophy of education, it was hard for him to realize his ideals. He therefore thought more and more of returning to the north.

Many of Confucius' students held office in Wei; they hoped that he would return to their state. In the ninth year of Duke Ai of Lu (486 B.C.), Confucius and his party left Fuhan and traveled through Chen and Song, and returned to Diqiu (in modern Puyang County, Henan Province), the state capital of Wei. At this time, the danger of the father and son struggling for power in Wei had just died down; the winner in this struggle was the son, not the father. The new lord, Duke Chu of Wei, wanted to invite Confucius to

贞子家。陈国君主陈湣（mǐn）公很快召见了孔子，他十分敬佩孔子的博学，将孔子视为尊贵的宾客。但是，在陈国的几年，孔子并没有能够实现自己的政治理想。公元前489年，吴国攻打陈国，楚国的楚昭王亲自出征来救，病死在军中，楚军被迫撤退，吴军攻到陈国都城宛丘城下，孔子一行便匆匆离开了宛丘。因吴、楚交战，粮食稀缺，孔子一行走到陈国和蔡国交界的地方已无粮可吃，陷于极度困难之中，弟子们也流露出不满情绪。尽管如此，孔子仍然镇静自若，讲诵弦歌不断，弟子们深受感染，最终度过了难关。孔子一行到达负函（今河南省信阳市）时，受到了楚国大夫沈诸梁（因为他的封地在叶这个地方，故被称为叶公）的热情款待，孔子与他讨论了政治问题，提出为政的理想境界在于使远方的人愿意来投奔，使近处的人更加亲近、团结。事后，叶公问孔子的学生子路：孔子是什么样的一个人？子路无法回答。孔子说："应该告诉他，我是一个发愤忘食，乐而忘忧，不知道自己快要老的人。"❶ 这是孔子对自己人生特征的总结，也是对学生们最好的教育与勉励。孔子游历了楚国，对楚国的风土人情、历史文化有了更多的感受。

孔子游历多年，虽然传播了学理，但政治理想却难以实现，于是有思乡北归之意。

孔子有多位弟子在卫国做官，他们都希望孔子回到卫国。鲁哀公九年（公元前486年），孔子一行从负函经过陈国、宋国，回到了卫国的国都帝丘（今河南省濮阳县）。这时，卫国父子争夺君位的风波刚刚平息，夺得君位的是儿子而不是父亲，新君卫出公有意请孔子参政。子路便问孔子，如果执政，将首先

❶ 见《论语·述而》。

❶ See "Shu'er," *Lunyu*.

hold office. So Zilu asked Confucius, if he were to hold office, what would he do first? Confucius answered, "I must first solve the problem of the rectification of names." Confucius said this not only because of the chaotic political situation in Wei, but also because Confucius had all along made it a consistent socio-political principle. The source of political chaos in Wei was the struggle between father and son; the complex nature of this contradiction derived from the fact that the father was a minister, but the son was the lord, so the relationships between lord and minster, father and son were all mixed up. Zilu, in his blunt manner, said, "Master, you miss the point! Why should names be rectified?" But Confucius severely berated Zilu in his response, "Zilu, how can you be so crude?" ❶ Confucius felt that the chaotic condition of relations between father and son, lord and minster in Wei created social instability. The purpose of rectifying names was, first of all, to correct these relationships, making the names match reality. When the lord followed the way of a lord, and a minister followed the way of a minister, this would achieve social stability. But Confucius' ideals contradicted greatly with reality in Wei. Therefore, when Confucius returned to Wei this time, although he was treated with ritual courtesy by Duke Chu of Wei, still the Duke did not invite him to "participate in government," nor did he "ask his advice about government." At this time, Confucius' disciple Ran You was the family steward of Ji Kangzi, who held power in the state. In the spring of the 11th year of Duke Ai of Lu (484 B.C.), Qi attacked Lu. Ran You led the victorious defense against the Qi troops. Ji Kangzi then asked Ran You, "Are your military talents inborn, or did you acquire them through learning?" Ran You said, "My knowledge of military matters was learned from Confucius." Ran You then praised Confucius's talents and virtue, saying, "If you employ Confucius, you will achieve good results; if you spread his thought among the people, then even the spirits will find nothing to criticize." Thereupon, Ji Kangzi asked Ran You whether he could get Confucius to return to the state. Ran You stated, "Just avoid listening to petty persons and do not ignore Confucius and then it would work." ❷ Ji Kangzi accepted Ran You's advice, and sent someone to invite Confucius with full ritual courtesy to return to the state. In the 11th year of Duke Ai of Lu (484 B.C.), Confucius and his party returned to Confucius' homeland of Lu after 14 years of wandering. This year, Confucius was 68 years old.

从何做起？孔子回答："必须首先解决端正名分的问题。"孔子这样说，既是因为卫国的政治混乱，也是孔子一贯坚持的社会政治原则。卫国政治混乱的根源是父子争斗，矛盾的复杂性是因为父为臣，子为君，君与臣、父与子的关系发生了混乱。率直的子路说："老师，您真是迂阔啊，这何必纠正呢？"但是，子路受到了孔子的严厉呵斥："子路，你怎么这样粗鲁！"❶孔子认为卫国的君臣、父子关系混乱，使社会产生动荡，端正名分的目的首先在于理顺卫国君臣父子的关系，使其名实相副，君尽君道，臣尽臣道，实现社会安宁。孔子的观念与卫国的现实有很大的矛盾，因此，孔子这次回到卫国，虽然受到了卫出公的礼遇，但卫出公既没有要他"为政"，也没有向他"问政"。这时，孔子的一名弟子冉有已经做了鲁国执政季康子的家臣，在鲁哀公十一年（公元前484年）春天，齐攻鲁，冉有率领鲁军战胜了齐军。季康子问冉有："你的军事才华是天生的，还是学习来的？"冉有说："我的军事知识是从孔子那里学来的。"冉有对孔子的才德予以高度评价，说："任用了孔子，就会有成就；将他的思想传之于百姓，就是让鬼神来评价也没有什么遗憾的。"于是季康子问冉有可否召孔子回国？冉有说："只要你不要听小人的话而冷淡孔子就可以了。"❷季康子听从了冉有的建议，派人带了厚礼聘请孔子回国。鲁哀公十一年（公元前484年），孔子一行终于结束了长达十四年的漂泊生涯，回到了家乡鲁国。这一年孔子六十八岁。

❶ 见《论语·子路》。
❷ 见《史记·孔子世家》。

❶ See "Zilu," *Lunyu*.
❷ See "The Hereditary House of Confucius," in the *Records of the Grand Historian*.

五 晚年归鲁

Chapter V Return to Lu Late in Life

After he returned to Lu Confucius was well received by both Duke Ai and Ji Kangzi, and was honored as the "Elder of the State." Nevertheless, Confucius was already 68 years old, therefore Lu was ultimately unable to employ Confucius, nor did Confucius seek office. Although at the time the state of Lu venerated Confucius, still, those in power mostly sought profit over humane government. For example, the Jisun clan wanted to levy more taxes, preparing to change the existing system of taxation known as the "qiu" tax into the more than double "field" tax system. He therefore sent Ran You to seek Confucius' opinion. But Confucius did never respond, so Ran You said, "You, master, are the 'Elder of the State,' and your views are necessary before we can implement this plan, so why don't you express yourself?" Confucius could not help expressing himself, but he did so privately, saying to Ran You, "The administration of government by a gentleman should be based on ritual, and should be undertaken for the common people. It should be balanced and reasonable and require little be taken from the common people. If done in this manner, then the 'qiu' system of taxation would be good enough. But if administration is not done according to ritual, then greed will become insatiable, and even if the 'field' type of taxation is implemented, they will not be satiated. If the Jisun clan administrates according to the law, then the laws and institutions from the time of the Duke of Zhou are still operative, and can be the legal basis for administration. But if he wants to collect taxes in an arbitrary manner, what need is there to consult me?" ❶ So Confucius opposed the "field" system of taxation, but Ji Kangzi and Ran You did not accept what Confucius advised, and started to implement it in the next year. This affair really shocked Confucius, especially the fact that the "field" system of taxation was implemented with the help of Ran You. Therefore, Confucius raged that "Ran Qiu is not my student! You disciples can rebuke him all you want!" ❷ This was the only time in his life that Confucius delivered such a severe rebuke to one of his own disciples.

Late in life, Confucius continued to participate in his educational activities; this made Confucius the happiest at this stage of his life. Confucius had many disciples; Sima Qian stated that among the disciples of Confucius "72 personally mastered the Six Classics." ❸ The editors of the *Analects* isolated four categories of outstanding achievement among his students: "Those outstanding in moral conduct included Yan Yuan, Min Ziqian, Ran Boniu, and Zhonggong. Those outstanding in speech were Zai Wo and Zigong. Those outstanding in political ability included Ran You and Jilu. Those outstanding

孔子回到鲁国后，虽然受到了鲁哀公和季康子的厚待，被尊称为国老，但是，孔子已经是六十八岁的老人了，因此，鲁国最终没有用孔子，孔子也不求为官。鲁国当时虽然对孔子十分尊崇，但当政者往往重利而轻仁，如，季孙氏想要多征赋税，准备改以前的"丘赋"为多一倍的"田赋"，便派冉有征求孔子意见，孔子一直不肯回答，冉有说："老师是国老，现在这件事需要您表态后才能施行。为什么老师您还不发表意见呢？"孔子最后不得已私下对冉有说："君子的行政，应该按礼而行，应当对百姓多施予，办事应适得其中，收取百姓的要少些。如果是这样，那么实行原有的'丘赋'就可以了。如果不按礼办事，贪得无厌，那么虽然实行了'田赋'，还会感到不满足的。如果季孙氏依法行事，那么周公时的法典还在，可以作为依据；如果想要随便收取赋税，那么你何必访求我呢？"❶"田赋"受到了孔子的反对，但季康子与冉有并没有听从孔子的劝告，而是从第二年就开始实施。此事使孔子深受刺激，尤其是"田赋"是在冉有的帮助之下实施的，因此，孔子愤怒地说："冉求不是我的学生！弟子们可以大张旗鼓地申斥他！"❷对学生如此严厉的批评，在孔子一生中仅此一次。

晚年的孔子，主要继续从事教育事业，这也是孔子晚年最为愉快的事。孔门弟子很多，司马迁说孔子弟子中"身通六艺者七十有二人"❸。《论语》的编者总结孔子弟子中出类拔萃的有四类："德行突出的有：颜渊、闵子骞、冉伯牛、仲弓。言语才能突出的有：宰我、子贡。政事才能突出的有：冉有、季

❶ 见《左传·哀公十一年》。

❷ 见《论语·先进》。

❸ 见《史记·孔子世家》。

❶ See "Duke Ai 11th year," *Zuozhuan*.

❷ See "Xianjin," *Lunyu*.

❸ See "The Hereditary House of Confucius," in the *Records of the Grand Historian*.

in classical learning were Ziyou and Zixia." ❶ Among these disciples were those who were "advanced first" and those who were "advanced later." To be "advanced first" meant those who accompanied Confucius in his wanderings among the various states, such as Yan Min, Zhonggong, and Zilu, et al. To be "advanced later" meant those students who came to Confucius after his return from his wanderings, such as Ziyou and Zixia, et al. Confucius felt that those who advanced first were more good-hearted and honest; those who advanced later were more meticulous in matter of the rites and musical performance. ❷ From this it is evident that disciples from different periods were different in terms of style and characteristics. The students from last period had outstanding talent that Confucius nurtured; their accomplishments were therefore great. Of course, Confucius late in life experienced the pain of losing disciples in death. Among the most painful were the deaths of Yan Yuan and Zilu.

Yan Yuan was Confucius' favorite disciple. His name was Hui, and style Ziyuan; he was also called Yan Yuan. He was younger than Confucius by 30 years; he died during the 14th year of Duke Ai of Lu (481 B.C.) at the age of 41. Confucius was devastated, and kept sighing that "Heaven wants to take my life!" He also said, "If one does not grieve for someone like this, who should one grieve for?" ❸ In the eyes of Confucius, Yan Yuan was naturally clever, hardworking and devoted to learning; he never transferred his anger to someone innocent, and never made the same mistake twice. Of the highest moral character, he was one who truly enacted the way of humaneness. Confucius said, "Yan Hui (Yan Yuan) could go a long time without transgressing the way of humaneness" ❹ ; he was different from Confucius' other disciples who only occasionally thought of humaneness. Yan Hui was at ease in poverty and happy following the way, and possessed of fine moral cultivation. Confucius said, "How worthy Hui is! He makes so with a bowl of rice, a gourd full of water, and lives in a shabby lane. He endures suffering that others cannot, yet is not moved from his happiness. Worthy, indeed, Hui is!" ❺ The meaning of this passage is that the virtuous person Yan Hui happily lives in a little lane, and is satisfied eating a bowl of rice and drinking a gourd of water. Yan Yuan was also Confucius' best student. Confucius said after Yan Yuan's death, "I had a disciple named Yan Yuan who was completely devoted to learning; unfortunately he died at an early age; there will be no more like him now." ❻ Although Confucius was devastated by Yan Yuan's death, he

路。文学才能突出的有：子游、子夏。"❶ 这些弟子中有先进，有后进。所谓先进，是指孔子周游列国前的弟子，如颜闵、仲弓、子路等人。后进则是出游归来后的弟子，如子游、子夏等人。孔子认为先进者较为淳厚质朴，而后进者对礼乐讲求细密。❷ 可见，不同时期的弟子，风格、特征也有所不同。这一时期孔子得英才而育之，成就很大。当然，晚年的孔子也时时有弟子去世的痛惜，其中最令孔子痛心的是颜渊与子路的死。

颜渊是孔子最得意的学生，名回，字子渊，也称颜渊，他比孔子小三十岁，鲁哀公十四年（公元前481年）四十一岁去世。孔子十分悲痛，连连叹息："这是老天爷要我的命啊！"并且说："不为这样的人伤心，还为什么人伤心呢？"❸ 在孔子眼里，颜渊天资聪慧，勤奋好学，不把怒气发泄到无关的人身上，不犯相同的错误，品格高尚，是仁道的真正实行者。孔子说："颜回能很长时间不违背仁德"❹，而与孔子的其他学生仅仅偶尔想起仁德不同。颜回安贫乐道，具有良好的道德修养，孔子说："贤哉，回也！一箪食，一瓢饮，在陋巷，人不堪其忧，回也不改其乐。贤哉，回也！"❺ 意思是贤人颜渊，愉快地居住在小巷，一竹筐饭，一瓢水就满足了。颜渊也是孔子最好学的弟子，孔子在颜渊去世后说过："我有个弟子叫颜回，十分好学，不幸早逝，现在再没有这样的人了。"❻孔子

❶ 见《论语·先进》。
❷ 见《论语·先进》。
❸ 见《论语·先进》。
❹ 见《论语·雍也》。
❺ 见《论语·雍也》。
❻ 见《论语·先进》。

❶ See "Xianjin," *Lunyu.*
❷ See "Xianjin," *Lunyu.*
❸ See "Xianjin," *Lunyu.*
❹ See "Yongye," *Lunyu.*
❺ See "Yongye," *Lunyu.*
❻ See "Xianjin," *Lunyu.*

advocated burying him according to ritual propriety. But the other disciples were also devastated by his death, and so buried him with full honors. Confucius did not interfere, but only stated, "Yan Hui regarded me as a father, but I cannot regard him as a son! Burying him with full honors was not my idea; it was something done by certain disciples!" ❶ Confucius' dilemma shows how he revered ritual requirements; but on the other hand, it embodies the depth of feelings that existed between master and his disciple and among all the students.

The second year after the death of Yan Yuan (the 15th year of Duke Ai of Lu, 480 B.C.), Zilu, another student whom Confucius was very fond of, died tragically. Zilu was surnamed Zhong, his name was You, and his style was Zilu. He was also known as Jilu, and was nine years younger than Confucius. Zilu was brave and upright, and was one of Confucius' most intimate disciples and friends. When Zilu was serving as the family steward to Kong Kui in the state of Wei, the heir apparent to the throne of Wei, Kuai Kui, secretly returned to Wei from his exile to launch a coup d'etat. Zilu did not heed the advice of others. Rather, he said, "If one is employed by someone, one shares his troubles." This means that if one receives a salary from another, then one should not leave when this person runs into difficulties. Thereupon, he risked his life by entering Diqiu, the capital of Wei. When rescuing Kong Kui, his chin strap was broken. Zilu then stated, "When a gentleman is about to die, he has to wear a cap." ❷ So he put on his chin strap, tightened it up, and died. Confucius greatly admired Zilu's bold and loyal character. When he died, it was yet another heavy blow to the aged Confucius.

Confucius in old age also suffered the bitterness of losing his wife and son. His wife Lady Qiguan died of illness the year before Confucius returned to Lu. Lady Qiguan had born one son and one daughter, and had administered the household and raised her children for decades. At the same time, Confucius' elder brother Mengpi was unable to take care of his children because of an affliction in his legs and feet, so Lady Qiguan had shouldered the responsibility for raising these nieces and nephews. Lady Qiguan was worried about Confucius' safety, especially while he was traveling abroad for 10-plus years. During the 13th year of Duke Ai of Lu (482 B.C.), unfortunately, Confucius' only son, Kong Li, died as well; he was only 50 years old. The deaths of his family members as well as the passing of one after another of his disciples were a continuous series of heavy blows. So during the spring of the

虽然十分伤痛，但对于颜渊的葬礼却主张依"礼"而行。弟子们对颜渊之死十分悲伤，还是厚葬了颜渊。对此，孔子并没有干预，只是说："颜回把我看作和他父亲一样，可是我却不能把他看作和儿子一样啊！厚葬不是我的主意，是若干弟子们一定要这样做的啊！"❶孔子的两难既可以看出他遵守礼法的一面，也体现了师生及同门之间情谊深厚的一面。

颜渊去世的第二年（鲁哀公十五年，公元前480年），孔子另一个十分喜爱的弟子子路又惨遭不幸。子路，姓仲，名由，字子路，也称为季路，比孔子小九岁。子路勇而有义，是孔子最亲密的弟子和朋友之一。子路在做卫国执政孔悝（kuī）的家臣时，流亡在外的卫国太子蒯聩（kuǎi kuì）秘密回到卫国，发动政变，子路不顾他人劝阻，他说："食其食者不避其难。"意思是说吃人家的俸禄，就不应该在人家危难时逃离。于是冒死进入卫国都城帝丘，营救孔悝，搏斗中子路的帽带被击断，子路说："君子临死时，不能不戴帽子。"❷他系紧帽带而死。孔子对子路勇毅忠诚的性格十分赞赏。子路的死，对晚年的孔子是又一次沉重的打击。

晚年的孔子还遭受了丧妻失子之痛。妻子亓官氏在孔子返回鲁国的前一年病故。亓官氏生一子一女，数十年操持家务，培养子女。同时，孔子的哥哥孟皮因腿脚有病，无力抚育子女，亓官氏还承担了养护侄女的义务。尤其是孔子漂泊在外十几年，亓官氏也为孔子的安全担忧。鲁哀公十三年（公元前482年），孔子唯一的儿子孔鲤也不幸去世，年仅五十岁。家庭不幸与弟子的先后辞世使晚年的孔子受到了一连串沉重的打击，鲁哀公

❶ 见《论语·先进》。
❷ 见《左传·哀公十五年》。

❶ See "Xianjin," *Lunyu*.
❷ See "Duke Ai 15th year," *Zuozhuan*.

16th year of Duke Ai of Lu (479 B.C.), Confucius, who was well up in years, was stricken by an illness. He felt that he was not long for this world. One day in the morning, Confucius grabbed his cane and stood unconcernedly at the front of his door, and sang out, "Towering Mt. Tai, you will soon collapse! Lofty rafters, you will soon snap! Brilliant sage, you will soon wither like the grass!" ❶ After chanting this, he entered and sat down facing the door. After hearing this, Zigong said, "Mt. Tai collapsing, lofty rafters snapping and the sage withering—what will we ever rely on in the future? Master, you most likely are ill, right?" Confucius answered, "I will probably die soon." After this, Confucius never got better. After about a week, this great sage stopped philosophizing forever. He was 73 years old.

Confucius gained great fame during his life, and was universally reverenced by commoners and aristocrats alike. After his death, Duke Ai of Lu personally composed a eulogy. It said, "Oh Blue Heaven, you are inhumane; why have you not spared us this 'Elder of the State,' letting him protect the state throne? I this lonely man have mourned so much that I am ill. Oh Confucius, your death is so tragic! I will never again have a sage to take for my model." ❷

After the death of Confucius and all the way through to the Han Dynasty, for more than 200 years Confucius was universally esteemed. When Han emperors went to Lu, they would sacrifice to Confucius with solemn ceremonies; whenever feudal princes or great ministers visited Qufu, they would often first visit Confucius' grave, and then they would conduct their political business. Afterwards, rulers and ministers throughout Chinese history would revere Confucius. During the reign of Emperor Wu of Han, the thought that Confucius had established monopolized the court, became the ruling ideology; it therefore profoundly influenced every level of Chinese political thought, moral ideals, and social psychology in history.

After Confucius' death, he was buried on the bank of Sishui River to the north of Qufu, the capital of the state of Lu. His disciples mourned him for three years. Zigong built a thatched hut at the side of the grave, and maintained a routine of mourning for six years. Such disciples as Zixia, Zizhang, and Ziyou et al. missed Confucius. They felt that among all of the disciples, You Ruo looked the most like Confucius, so they wanted to follow him just as they had Confucius in order to relieve their feelings of longing. But Zengzi said, "This

十六年（公元前479年）春天，年迈的孔子病倒了。孔子感到他将不久于人世，一天早上，孔子扶着手杖，意态逍遥地站立在门前，歌叹道："巍巍泰山啊，快要崩颓！高高的梁木啊，快要断折！炯炯的哲人啊，快要像草木那样枯萎了！"❶唱过之后进门当户而坐。子贡听到后，说："泰山崩颓，我们哪里还有崇仰的圣山，高高的梁木、炯炯的哲人颓萎，我们将何以依傍啊？老师，您大概病了吧？"孔子说："大概我快要死了。"从此一病不起。大约一个星期之后，这位伟大的圣哲停止了思想，时年七十三岁。

孔子生前已获得了巨大的声誉，得到了君臣百姓的普遍敬重。孔子去世后，鲁哀公亲自写文表示哀悼，他说："苍天啊，你真的不仁善，为什么不留下这一国老，让他保护我的君位。我孤单一人，悲伤成病。孔子啊，（你的去世）我是多么悲哀啊！从此我再也没有师法的标准了。"❷

孔子去世后，直到汉代，二百多年中受到了普遍的推尊。汉代的皇帝到鲁地，用隆重的仪式祭祀孔子，诸侯大臣到曲阜，也常常是先拜谒孔子陵墓，然后再从事政事。此后的历代君臣都对孔子十分崇敬，汉武帝时，孔子所创立的儒家思想更被朝廷独尊，成为统治思想，深深地影响了中国历代政治观念、道德理想与社会心理等各个层面。

孔子死后，被安葬在鲁国都城曲阜北部的泗水之滨。弟子们守丧三年，子贡则在墓旁筑草屋，守丧达六年之久。子夏、子张、子游等弟子思念孔子，他们觉得弟子中有若容貌像孔子，便想把有若当作孔子侍奉，以解思念之情。曾子说："这不行，

❶ 见《礼记·檀弓上》。
❷ 见《左传·哀公十六年》。

❶ See "Tangong," Part One, the *Rites*.
❷ See "Duke Ai 16th year," *Zuozhuan*.

will not work. Our master was like a surging river current flowing by, gleaming incomparably white in the hot sun of summer; no one could possibly compare with him." ❶

Later generations came to pay homage to Confucius in an endless flow, and planted pine and cypress trees around his tomb. This gradually formed a cemetery grove of quite large proportions; it was called the "Confucian Grove." Some disciples and people from Lu moved next to the grave to live in order to honor Confucius in their memories. Thereafter, this quarter became known as "Confucius' Quarter." Two years after the death of Confucius, Duke Ai of Lu changed the name of Confucius' former residence to that of "The Confucian Temple." Confucius' descendants then selected places for their own residences, what is now known as "The Confucian Compound."

老师就像滔滔的江水洗过，夏日的骄阳晒过，洁白光明无比啊，谁也不可与他相比啊。"❶

后代拜谒孔子的人络绎不绝，在孔子墓周围种植很多松柏，逐渐形成了规模很大的孔氏陵园，称为"孔林"；有些弟子和鲁国人因为追念孔子，搬到孔子的墓旁住下，于是就把这里叫做"孔里"；孔子去世后第二年，鲁哀公就将孔子生前居住的房舍改称为"孔庙"；孔子的后代则另外选择居住的地方，就是现在的"孔府"。

❶ 见《孟子·滕文公上》。

❶ See "Tengwengong," Part One, *Mencius*.

孔府和孔林

Confucian Compound and Confucian Grove

六　"敬天命而远之"——孔子的宗教观

Chapter Ⅵ　" Honor Heavenly Fate yet Keep It at a Distance" : Confucius' Religious View

The ancient Chinese view of religion was often closely connected to the Way of Heaven. It is very significant for the understanding of the basic nature of Confucius' thought and of the thought of ancient China to learn how to understand Confucius' view on the Way of Heaven. Although Confucius' view seems to be ambiguous, it actually was quite unique to himself, and exerted an important influence on the development of Chinese thought. Confucius' religious view was manifested mainly in his theories on heavenly fate, and ghosts and spirits.

Let's first discuss his view on heavenly fate. When the *Analects* mentions "heaven," it has complicated connotations. On the one hand, it implies a "heaven with a volition." For instance, "The only one who understands me is heaven." ❶ It is obvious that this "heaven" implies an anthropomorphic spirit. Confucius once expressed his awe of the Way of Heaven. He said, "If one offends heaven, then it is of no use to pray." ❷ It is clear that "heaven" is an anthropomorphic spirit that can understand human affairs and has the ability to punish. On the other hand, "heaven" also carries the implication of "heaven as nature," just as Confucius said, "Truly lofty! Only heaven is so high, and only the ancient sage-kings of legend were able to imitate heaven." ❸ What Confucius was sighing about was that Yao possessed a greatness of form similar to "heaven." Therefore, "heaven" in this sense implies "heaven as nature." At the same time, Confucius used two approaches to rid "heavenly fate" of its mystical qualities.

One of these approaches was to unite "heaven" with the human realm and to emphasize the relationship between heaven and the human individual, for heaven bequeathed "virtue" to man. When the people of Kuang confused Confucius with Yang Hu and incarcerated him, Confucius said, "If heaven does not wish to destroy culture, then what can the people of Kuang do to me?" ❹ When Confucius discussed "heaven," he sacralized "this culture" that he had inherited together with the "virtue" inherently within him. This is entirely in keeping with his view on the Way of Humaneness. In other words, his Way of Heaven derived from his ethical thinking that was based on humaneness. What this signified was that "heaven" was no longer a completely mysterious power beyond human affairs that controlled mankind; instead it possessed human qualities.

中国古代的宗教观往往与天道观联系在一起，如何认识孔子的天道观，对于理解孔子和中国古代思想的基本品质具有重要的意义。孔子的天道观虽然看似模棱两可，其实具有自己的特色，并对中国思想文化的发展有重要的影响。孔子的宗教观主要体现为他的天命观与鬼神论。

先说天命观。《论语》中所说的"天"具有较复杂的内涵。一方面有"意志之天"的含义，如，"了解我的，只有天吧"❶。显然这个"天"具有人格神的意味。孔子也曾对天道表示过敬畏，他说："得罪了上天，祈祷也没有用。"❷ 可见，"天"是可以知晓人事并具有惩戒功能的人格神。另一方面，"天"也有"自然之天"的含义，如孔子所说的"真的崇高啊！只有天最大，只有传说中的远古帝王尧能效法天"❸。孔子感叹的是尧具有与"天"相似的形体之大，因此，这里的"天"当是指"自然之天"。同时，孔子还从两个途径去除了"天"、"命"的神秘色彩：

一是将"天"与人道结合在一起，注重天与人个体之间的关系，天授人以"德"。当孔子被匡人误当作阳虎拘禁起来时，孔子说："天如果不想消灭文化，那匡人能把我怎么样呢？"❹ 孔子论"天"，将内在的"德"和他自己传承的"斯文"神圣化，这与他的仁道观念一致。也就是说，他的天道是从属于以仁为本的伦理思想的。从这个意义上说，"天"不再完全是人类之外并主宰人类的神奇力量，而具有了人性的色彩。

❶ 见《论语·宪问》。
❷ 见《论语·八佾》。
❸ 见《论语·泰伯》。
❹ 见《论语·子罕》。

❶ See "Xianwen," *Lunyu*.
❷ See "Bayi," *Lunyu*.
❸ See "Taibo," *Lunyu*.
❹ See "Zihan," *Lunyu*.

　　The second approach was to rationalize "heaven," to regard it as a force of nature. As Confucius said, "What does heaven say? The four seasons operate as always, all things grow as always, so what does heaven say?" ❶ This implies that the way nature operates was the same as the Way of Heaven; no longer was the Way of Heaven a mysterious force. Instead, it was a natural principle with its own set of rules, so the Way of Heaven now became rationalized.

　　What is worth noticing is that the way Confucius explained the "Way of Heaven" incorporated the aspects of both "operation" and "creation and growth"; that is, to Confucius, the Way of Heaven was manifested as a dynamic process. The significance of this is that, when Confucius said "heaven created this virtue in me," this was nothing exceptional in that "heaven" was a universal principle in the natural process of life and of organisms. Therefore, "heaven" was no anthropomorphic sovereign spirit in the religious sense; rather, it was a function that included both "operation" and "creation and growth." Although Confucius did not offer a systematic and clear exposition of this, still his views removed the sacred aspects of "heaven," and opened up the connection between "heaven" and "humanity." The significance of this is that Confucius' thoughts in this regard are quite close to Daoist thinking.

　　Confucius linked "heaven" with "fate," and devalued the anthropomorphism of "heaven," like when Zixia heard Confucius say "Life and death are due to fate, but wealth and status are due to heaven." ❷ Confucius linked "heaven" with "fate," and both clearly signified similar things. "Fate" generally indicates the power that controls social life. Confucius said, "If one does not understand objective fate, then one cannot become a gentleman." ❸ This obviously is very different from the unreserved worship of an anthropomorphic spirit. Confucius said, "When I was 50 I knew the fate of heaven." ❹ This is not saying to worship heavenly fate, rather, to understand "heaven" and "fate," in other words, to realize an objective power that cannot be contravened. Confucius linked "heaven" with "fate," endowing "heaven" with an objective and inevitable connotation. Confucius also stated, "The gentleman fears three things; he fears heavenly fate, he fears great men, and he

二是将"天"理性化，将其视为自然的力量，如他说："天说了什么吗？四季照常运行，百物照常生长，天说了什么吗？"❶ 这里隐含着将自然运行之道与天道统一的意味，天道不再是神秘的力量，而是有规律的自然法则，天道具有了理性的色彩。

值得注意的是，孔子论述了"天道"具有"行"与"生"的属性，也就是说，在孔子这里，天道展示的是一种动态的过程，从这个意义上说，孔子说"天生德于予"并不是一个特例，而是"天"作为生命、生物过程的普遍法则，因此，"天"就不是宗教意义上具有主体性的人格神，而是具有"行"与"生"的功能。对此，孔子虽然没有进行系统明确的阐述，但是他的观点消解了"天"的神性，打通了"天"与"人"之间的联系。从这个意义上说，孔子的思想又与道家思想颇有相通之处。

孔子将"天"与"命"并列起来，也淡化了"天"的人格神色彩。如子夏曾听孔子说过"死生有命，富贵在天"❷。孔子将"命"与"天"并列，两者显然具有相似的意义。"命"一般都是指支配社会生活的力量，孔子说："不知道客观的'命'就不能成为君子。"❸ 这与无条件地敬奉人格神具有明显的区别。孔子说"五十而知天命"❹，并不是说崇信天之命，而是知道"天"与"命"，就是知晓客观的不可违逆的力量。孔子将"天"与"命"并列，赋予了"天"客观必然性的含义。孔子还说过："君子有三件畏惧的事情：畏惧天命，畏惧大人，

❶ 见《论语·阳货》。
❷ 见《论语·颜渊》。
❸ 见《论语·尧曰》。
❹ 见《论语·为政》。

❶ See "Yang Huo," *Lunyu*.
❷ See "Yan Yuan," *Lunyu*.
❸ See "Yaoyue," *Lunyu*.
❹ See "Weizheng," *Lunyu*.

fears the words of the sages." ❶ Confucius linked heavenly fate, great men, and words of sages together, demonstrating the interaction between heaven and humanity, endowing "heaven" with human qualities. Therefore, "To understand heavenly fate" and "heaven created virtue in me," both embody the theory of the unity of heaven and humanity from different angles.

Confucius linked "heaven" with "fate," or discussed "fate" as an independent entity, and also endowed "fate" and "Heaven" with meanings that were not completely similar: "Heaven" is the symbol of virtue and human nature; "fate" is a kind of intangible power. Because of the role of "fate," neither goodness, righteousness, nor even evil are able to decide success or failure. From this point of view, "fate" is the supplement to the "Way of Heaven," a supplemental explanation resulting from the fact that the phenomenon of the virtue of Heaven lacked any efficacy. For example, Confucius' student Ran Boniu became gravely ill, so Confucius went to see him. Confucius grasped Boniu's hand through the window and said, "It will be hard for him to survive; this is fate! For such a man to contract such an illness! For such a man to contract such an illness!" ❷ Confucius could not understand how Boniu could contract such a serious illness and felt a lot of pain. Confucius felt that this was the role of "fate." Therefore, Confucius admitted that: "Will the Great Way be realized? Perhaps it will be decided by fate. Will the Great Way be abandoned? Perhaps it will be decided by fate." ❸ In other words, the success or failure of righteous and good deeds are all decided by fate.

Confucius' understanding of "fate" was that one must "know fate," which is to accept "fate" and not try to change it. Only in this way can one be a "gentleman." Of course, Confucius' attitude towards those matters that are determined by "heaven" or "fate" was that "things that obviously cannot be done still have to be done." ❹ But this does not mean that one must change the limits imposed by "fate" ; he was merely expressing his self-conscious expectations. As for these views of Confucius, the explanation from his student Zilu was: "When a gentleman emerges to take up a government post,

畏惧圣人的语言。"❶孔子将天命、大人、圣人之言相并列，显示了天与人之间的互通，赋予了"天"人性化的色彩。因此，"知天命"与"天生德于予"从不同的角度体现了天人合一的理论取向。

孔子将"天"与"命"并列，或者将"命"作为独立的范畴来讨论，也赋予了"命"与"天"不尽相同的含义："天"是道德、人性的象征，"命"则是指一种不可捉摸的力量。由于"命"的作用，善良、正义还是邪恶并不能决定成和败。从这个意义上说，"命"是"天道"的补充，是对天德并无灵验报应的现象作出的补充解释。比如，孔子的学生冉伯牛病危，孔子去探问，从窗户里握着伯牛的手说："难得活了，这是命呀！这样的人竟生这样的病！这样的人竟生这样的病！"❷ 对伯牛生如此重的病十分不解与痛惜，孔子认为，这是"命"的作用。因此，孔子承认："大道将实现吗？是命决定的；大道将废除吗？也是命决定的。"❸就是说，正义的、善良的事成功或失败，都由命运决定。

孔子对于"命"的认识，是要"知命"，就是承认"命"而不是改变"命"，只有这样才是"君子"。当然，孔子对于"天"与"命"所注定的事情，也曾经认为"明知办不到也要去办"❹，但这并不是他希望改变"命"的限制，仅仅是表达自觉的愿望而已。对于孔子的这些观念，他的学生子路的解释是："君子出来做官，只是尽应尽之责。大道行不通，已经早

❶ 见《论语·季氏》。
❷ 见《论语·雍也》。
❸ 见《论语·宪问》。
❹ 见《论语·宪问》。

❶ See "Jishi," *Lunyu.*
❷ See "Yongye," *Lunyu.*
❸ See "Xianwen," *Lunyu.*
❹ See "Xianwen," *Lunyu.*

he should do his best at his duties; if the Great Way cannot be implemented, he already knows this in advance." ❶

Now let's move to Confucius' views on ghosts and spirits. Confucius' views are actually contradictory. On the one hand, he perhaps had views that he did not express; or perhaps he respected ghosts and sprits but kept away from them. Confucius usually avoided speaking about them. It says in the *Analects*, "Confucius did not discuss strange marvels, brave feats of strength, rebellions, or ghosts and spirits." ❷ His attitude towards ghosts and spirits was ambiguous and doubtful. When Confucius' student Zilu asked him how to serve ghosts and spirits, Confucius responded: "If one cannot serve humanity, how can one serve ghosts and spirits?" Zilu asked further, "May I be so bold as to inquire about death?" Confucius said, "If we do not understand the way of life, how can we understand death?" ❸ It is apparent that Confucius was concerned about the practical matters of life; as for death, and ghosts and spirits, he did his best to avoid them. On the other hand, Confucius did mention reverencing ghosts and spirits and sacrificing to them. Once when Confucius' student Fan Chi asked what was "wisdom," Confucius responded, "To honor ghosts and spirits but avoid them, this may be called wisdom." ❹ He also said, "It is flattery to sacrifice to a spirit or ghost that one should not sacrifice to." ❺ This statement apparently concedes the existence of ghosts and spirits. Confucius was unclear on this topic, but even though he did not deny the existence of ghosts and spirits, during an age when the power witchcraft was ascendant, Confucius intentionally avoided discussing ghosts and spirits. He regarded avoiding the topic as the best policy. This shows that he was doubtful concerning them, and in some respects denied their existence.

Confucius advocated "reverencing ghosts and spirits," and placed great emphasis on sacrificial ceremonies. This was because Confucius respected the practice of filial piety, sacrificing to ancestors, remembering the founder of the clan—all manifestations of the practice of filial piety, and they all naturally reveal human sentiments. Confucius's student Zai Wo once said to Confucius that the three-year mourning period after the death of one's parents was too long; one year should suffice. Confucius answered him, saying that if you start eating white rice and wearing garments of brocade within three years after the deaths of your parents, would you feel at ease in your heart? Confucius was

知道了。"❶

再说鬼神论。对于鬼神，孔子的看法有些矛盾。一方面，孔子对其或存而不论，或敬而远之。孔子平时回避说鬼神，《论语》中说："孔子不谈怪异、勇力、叛乱、鬼神。"❷他对鬼神含糊其辞，持犹疑的态度。孔子的学生子路问如何服事鬼神，孔子说："活人还不能服事，怎么能去服事死人？"子路又说："我斗胆请问死是怎么回事？"孔子说："生的道理还没有弄明白，怎么能够知道死？"❸可见，孔子关注的是现实人生，对于鬼神、生死问题尽量回避。另一方面，孔子也谈到对鬼神当敬之、祭之。当孔子的学生樊迟问什么是"智"时，孔子说："尊敬鬼神而远避他们，可以说是智了。"❹又说："不应该祭祀的鬼神而去祭它，这是谄媚（chǎn mèi)啊。"❺这似乎是承认鬼神的存在。尽管孔子在鬼神问题上的表述似乎有些飘忽不定，其实孔子虽然没有否认鬼神，但在巫鬼势力旺盛的时代，孔子刻意避免讨论鬼神，将远避鬼神问题视为聪明的表现，可见他对鬼神是怀疑的，颇有几分否认的意味。

孔子主张"敬鬼神"，并且对于祭祀活动也十分重视。这一方面是因为孔子崇尚孝道，祭奠先人，追思远祖，是孝道的表现，也是情感的自然流露。孔子的学生宰我曾对孔子说，父母去世后，守孝三年时间太长了，一年就可以了。孔子回答说，父母去世不到三年，你吃白米饭，穿花缎衣，能心安吗？对于

❶ 见《论语·微之》。
❷ 见《论语·述而》。
❸ 见《论语·先进》。
❹ 见《论语·雍也》。
❺ 见《论语·为政》。

❶ See "Weizhi," *Lunyu*.
❷ See "Shu' er," *Lunyu*.
❸ See "Xianjin," *Lunyu*.
❹ See "Yongye," *Lunyu*.
❺ See "Weizheng," *Lunyu*.

very upset with Zai Wo feeling good about mourning for only one year, and considered him to be inhumane; this is because after children are born, they only leave the side of their parents after three years. Therefore, it is entirely reasonable that mourning one's parents for three years is a universal practice. This is also the reason that Confucius emphasized funerary sacrifices. At the same time, sacrificial ceremonies aided the development of good social morals. Confucius' disciple Zengzi said: "Be mindful of attending to the end of life and of seeking after your ancestors and the people will be good at moral conduct." ❶ This means that one should carefully attend to the deaths of one's parents, ever remember one's ancestors, and magnify the Way of Filial Piety; this will lead to good morals among the people. On the other hand, reverencing ghosts and spirits, emphasizing sacrificial ceremonies, and holding one's ancestors in fond memory will cause the people to transcend the realities of existence in their thinking and thereby make their individual lives of transcendental significance. Therefore, even though Confucius' emphasis on sacrificial ceremonies partook of a religious significance, still at base it was concerned with practicalities.

To summarize the above, Confucius' views on "heavenly fate" and "ghosts and spirits" are strikingly different from religious theology. Mohists criticized Confucians for "believing that Heaven is aware, but ghosts and spirits are not." ❷ Confucius' view of religion is precisely like what Mr. Zhou Yutong said, "Confucius' philosophy emphasized moral cultivation within the human realm, therefore he did not discuss the questions of pre-existence or life after death, or of ghosts or spirits." ❸ American scholar Hebert Fingarette also stated, "Confucius said that neither human morality nor spiritual accomplishments depended on the intervention of spirits who either deceive or bless, nor do they depend on mysterious spells or any purely external force. This type of thinking takes an additional step in deepening the practical, this-world qualities of humanism represented in the *Analects*." ❹ The strong humanism embodied by Confucius' religious view exerted an important influence on Chinese culture.

宰我居丧一年而心安,孔子十分不满,认为宰我不仁,因为儿女出生之后,三年才可离开父母怀抱,因此,为父母守孝三年为天下通例,是完全合理的。这也是孔子重视丧葬祭祀的原因。同时,祭祀活动还有助于形成良好的社会风气。孔子的弟子曾子说:"慎终追远,民德归厚。"❶ 意思是说谨慎地对待父母的亡故,追念远祖,发扬孝悌之道,可导致民风淳厚。另一方面,敬鬼神,重祭祀,还可以通过对祖先的追怀,使人们产生超越现实生命的联想,从而使个体的生命具有无限的意义,因此,孔子重祭祀虽然具有宗教意味,但本质还是对现实的关注。

综上所述,孔子"天命"、"鬼神"的观念与宗教神学具有明显的区别,墨家批评儒家"认为天不神明,认为鬼不灵"❷。孔子的宗教观,诚如周予同先生所说的那样:"孔子的哲学只是着重人世间的道德陶冶,所以他不谈生前死后的鬼神问题,因此,他并不是一位宗教家。"❸ 美国学者芬格莱特(Herbert Fingarette)也说:"孔子认为,人类的道德和精神成就并不依靠欺骗或者幸运之神的降临,也不依赖于神秘的咒语或者任何纯粹外在的力量。这种思想进一步加深了《论语》现世的、务实的人文主义色彩。"❹ 孔子宗教观中体现出的强烈的人文色彩,对中国文化产生了重要的影响。

❶《论语·学而》。
❷ 见《墨子·公孟》。
❸《孔子》,载《周予同经学史论著选集》。
❹《孔子:即凡而圣》,江苏人民出版社 2002 年版,第2~3页。

❶ "Xue'er," *Lunyu*.
❷ See "Gongmeng," *Mozi*.
❸ "Confucins," in *Selections of Mr. Zhou Yutong on the History of Classical Scholarship*.
❹ *Confucius: The Secular as Sacred*. Nanjing: Jiangsu People's Press, 2002, pp. 2-3.

春秋时期文字：眉县大鼎铭文
Chinese characters in the Spring and Autumn
Period inscription on the Ding of Mei County

七 "仁者爱人"——孔子的道德哲学

Chapter Ⅶ " The Humane Person Loves Others" :
Confucius' Moral Philosophy

The core of Confucius' thought and its chief characteristic is moral philosophy; "humaneness," together with the related concept of "ritual," is the core of Confucius' moral philosophy.

First is about views concerning "humaneness." Confucius mainly treated the content of "humaneness," the path to achieving "humaneness," and the relationship between "humaneness" and the development of character.

First of all, let's discuss the content of "humaneness." Confucius regarded "humaneness" as one of the cardinal virtues. He said, "To be humane is to be human." When his student Fan Chi asked him about the definition of humaneness, he simply stated "love others" and "broadly love the masses." Of course, when he said "love others" he made certain distinctions. He said, "To be humane is to be human; the best is to be close to one's relatives." ❶ This means that it is the most important to love one's relatives. Confucius' student You Ruo also said, the foundation of "humaneness" was being filial towards one's parents and loving and respecting one's elder brothers. Confucius' student Zai Wo felt that mourning one's parents for three years was too long. But Confucius did not berate him for not being "filial" ; instead he said that he was "inhumane." This shows that "humaneness" included the virtue of "filial piety," and that "filial piety" was the root of "humaneness." "Humaneness" is the overarching principle in Confucius' moral philosophy. It contains various kinds of moral sub-categories; in addition to filial piety, the root of "humaneness," it also contains such moral categories as "wisdom" and "bravery." Zizhang asked Confucius about Lingyin Ziwen, who three times served in the government and three times was dismissed from office, yet never expressed happiness or distress whatever happened, and Chen Wenzi, who left states that were controlled by great officials; were these instances of the virtue of "humaneness" ? Confucius felt that although they could be called "loyal" and could claim "integrity," still they did not even come up to the level of "wise," much less that of "humane." We can see that "humaneness" contained "wisdom." Confucius further stated that the humane were definitely brave, but the brave were not necessarily humane, so "humanness" also contained "bravery."

"Humaneness" was not only rich in content, it furthermore was at the core of Confucius' system of thought. Well, was there any fundamental principle that permeated this system of thought based on "humaneness" ? Concerning this, Confucius once told his student Zeng Shen, "My way has one thread that

道德哲学是孔子思想的核心与重要特征，"仁"以及与其相关的"礼"又是孔子道德哲学的核心。这里分别叙述如下。

一、关于"仁"。孔子主要讨论了"仁"的内涵、"仁"的实现途径以及"仁"与人格培养的关系等。

首先，"仁"的内涵。孔子将"仁"看作人的基本品格，他说："仁者，人也。"当他的学生樊迟问什么是仁时，他简要地解释为"爱人"、"泛爱众"。当然，孔子的"爱人"也是有区别的，他说："仁者，人也，亲亲为大。"❶意思是爱自己的亲人最为重要。孔子的学生有若也说过：孝顺爹娘，敬爱兄长，就是"仁"的基础。孔子的学生宰我认为，为父母守丧三年时间太长，对此，孔子并没有责备他"不孝"，而是说他"不仁"，可见"仁"含有"孝"德，并且"孝"德是仁的根本。"仁"是孔子道德哲学的总纲领，它蕴涵了多种其他的道德子目，除了作为仁德根本的孝德之外，还包含"智"、"勇"等道德范畴。子张问孔子：令尹子文三次从政，三次被罢，而无喜无怒，陈文子几次离开大夫专权的国家，是否具有仁德？孔子认为，他们虽然可以称得上"忠"，可以称得上"清"，但还算不上"智"，哪里能谈得上"仁"？可见"仁"包含"智"。孔子还说过，仁者必定勇，勇者不一定仁，"仁"又包含了"勇"。

既然"仁"具有丰富的内涵，并且是孔子思想体系的核心，那么是否有贯穿孔子思想体系的"仁"的基本范畴呢？对此，孔子曾告诉他的学生曾参说："吾道一以贯之。"就是说，孔子

❶《礼记·中庸》。

❶ "Zhongyong," *Liji*.

permeates the whole." This is to say, Confucius' thought had a main principle that ran throughout it; this main thread, according to the understanding of Zeng Shen, was the way of "loyalty" and "reciprocity." Confucius said further, "Now as for the humane person, he desires to establish himself and to establish others, and he desires to realize himself and to realize others." ❶ "He desires to establish himself and to establish others, and he desires to realize himself and to realize others." This is "loyalty." This means that whenever one desires something for himself, he should think of how to help others to satisfy this same desire. The phrase "Whatever one does not desire, one should not impose on others" means "reciprocity." That is, the way one hopes others will not use to treat us, should not be used to treat others. Therefore, "loyalty" and "reciprocity" are two sides of the same coin, and their common ethical basis is "humaneness" ; both "loyalty" and "reciprocity" are the manifestations of the "Way of Humaneness." Yet "loyalty and reciprocity" are the "direction of humaneness." ❷ This is to say that "loyalty and reciprocity" are the yardsticks with which to measure humaneness. In order to achieve "loyalty and reciprocity," and to manifest the moral standards of "humaneness," it is necessary to measure others against ourselves, to regard others as ourselves, to eliminate private desires, and to maintain an impartial mind.

Next is the achievement of "humaneness." Confucius discussed even more the path towards achieving humaneness. Confucius felt that the virtue of humaneness was not something far off: "When I think of humaneness, it is here!" "To achieve the virtue of humaneness, does it depend on oneself or on others?" ❸ At the same time, Confucius believed that in order to gain "humaneness," it was necessary to integrate the learning of external knowledge with the cultivation of inner virtues. For instance, Confucius' disciple Zixia said, "To be broad of learning and profound in will, to inquire with modesty and to ponder in detail, humaneness is within these." ❹ This means to broadly acquire knowledge and to steadfastly maintain the will, to earnestly inquire after things, and to ponder over the problem of achieving humaneness, for the spirit of humaneness is found in this process. Confucius' students asked him how to achieve humaneness; he required them to be upright and serious, to perform each task assiduously and conscientiously, and to be loyal and sincere towards others at usual times. Likewise, when one disciple, Zhonggong, asked about humaneness, Confucius also said, when you exited you

的思想有贯彻始终的主线，这个主线按照孔子弟子曾参的理解就是"忠恕"之道。孔子又说："夫仁者，己欲立而立人，己欲达而达人。能近取譬，可谓仁之方也已。"❶ "己欲立而立人，己欲达而达人"就是"忠"，意思是说自己有什么欲求，要想着别人也有这样的欲求，在满足自己欲求的时候，要想着使别人也能满足这样的欲求；"己所不欲，勿施于人"就是"恕"，意思是说自己不愿别人这样对待我，我也不要这样对待别人。因此，"忠"与"恕"是二位一体的关系，其共同的伦理基础就是"仁"，"忠"与"恕"是"仁道"的体现。而"忠恕"又是"仁之方也"❷，就是说"忠恕"是衡量"仁"的尺度。实现"忠恕"，体现"仁"的道德标准，就需要以己度人，视人如己，清除私欲，具有大公之心。

其次，"仁"的实现。孔子讨论得更多的是实现"仁"的途径。孔子认为，仁德并不遥远，"我想仁，仁就到了！""实现仁德，全凭自己，还靠别人吗？"❸同时，孔子也认为，"仁"的获得还需要通过学习外在的知识与内在的修养相结合。如，孔子的弟子子夏说："博学而笃志，切问而近思，仁在其中矣。"❹ 意思是说广泛地学习知识，坚守自己的志趣，恳切地提问，多考虑现实的问题，仁的精神就在这一过程中。孔子的学生问孔子怎样做到仁，孔子要求他们平时要端正庄严，做事严肃认真，对人忠心诚意。同样，弟子仲弓问仁时，孔子也

❶《论语·雍也》。
❷《论语·雍也》。
❸ 见《论语·颜渊》。
❹《论语·子张》。

❶ "Yongye," *Lunyu.*
❷ "Yongye," *Lunyu.*
❸ See "Yan Yuan," *Lunyu.*
❹ "Zizhang," *Lunyu.*

should act as if greeting an honored guest; when governing the people you should act like going to assume responsibility for the performance of a grand sacrifice. In both instances you should be serious and conscientious, meticulous and prudent. He also advocated starting from respect, reverence, loyalty, and trustworthiness when cultivating the virtue of humaneness. All in all, cultivating the virtue of humaneness requires beginning from self-mastery, and assiduous effort to ultimately bring about the universal spread of the virtue of humaneness. This is what Confucius meant by "Overcome the self and return to the rites; when this is one day achieved, then the whole world will return to humaneness." ❶

The highest realm of humaneness is when it extends from family out to society; this is then the process of becoming a "sage." A "sage" is one who is able to aid the entire world. "The one who is able to transform the people on a great scale is called a sage." This means that the sage person needs to possess the ability to improve public morals, and that the highest goal of the sage person is to "comfort the people," "broadly love them," and "aid the masses." To Confucius, being able to aid the entire world and to comfort the people is a stage difficult to reach within the ideal realm of "humaneness" ; it is hard even for a sage. Twice in the *Analects* Confucius mentioned things that would possibly be hard for even Yao or Shun to do; these were what Zigong said about "finding good situations for the people on a large scale, and be able to help the masses," that is, "broadly ministering to the people and being able to save the masses" ❷ and the remarks that Confucius himself said "Cultivate oneself in order to comfort the people." ❸ From this we may see that the ultimate goal and highest realm of Confucius' orientation of advocating a personality of complete humaneness and complete sagacity was to save the world and comfort the people. The ideal personality advocated by Confucius actually proceeded from "humaneness" to "sagacity" directly to "broadly ministering" and "saving the masses." Of course, Confucius already granted the moral orientation to achieve this goal at the stage of cultivating the self for perfect virtue. The concept of "cultivating oneself in order to comfort the people" that he hoped for fully expressed this characteristic. The so-called term "self-cultivation" is cultivating the virtue of humaneness; "comforting the people" is its conclusion. Therefore, when he was judging whether or not others possessed the virtue of "humaneness," he often used the standard of whether or not they possessed this moral orientation. Confucius did not lightly grant "humaneness" to anyone in judging them. When somebody stated that Ran Yong possessed the virtue of humaneness despite lacking eloquence

说：出门如同见到贵宾，治民就如同去承担大祀典，都应当严肃认真，小心谨慎，主张修仁德当从恭、敬、忠、信入手。总之，修仁德需从克制自己、认真修持开始，最终实现仁德的普世化，这就是孔子所说的："克己复礼为仁，一日克己复礼，天下归仁焉。" ❶

"仁"的最高境界是由家庭扩展到社会，这也就是成"圣"的过程。"圣"是指能兼济天下的人，"大而化之之谓圣"，就是说，圣人需具有化民成俗的能力，圣人追求的最高目标是"安百姓"、"博施"、"济众"。在孔子看来，兼济天下、惠安百姓是难以企及的"仁"的理想境界，即使是圣人也不易做到。在《论语》中，孔子两次谈到尧、舜可能都难以做到的事情，这就是子贡所说的"广泛地给民众以好处，又能帮助民众"，即"博施于民而能济众" ❷，以及孔子自己所说的"修己以安百姓" ❸。可见，孔子所倡导的成仁、成圣的人格取向，最终的目的和最高的境界是济世安民。孔子倡导的理想人格其实是由"仁"而及"圣"直至"博施"、"济众"。当然，孔子在修己成仁的阶段已赋予了实现这一最高目标的价值取向，他所期盼的"修己以安百姓"，就充分表达了这一特征。所谓"修己"就是修养仁德，"安百姓"是归宿。因此，他在评价人们是否具有"仁"德时，往往也以是否具有这一取向为标准。孔子并不轻易用"仁"来评价他人。当有人说冉雍有仁德而没有口才

❶ 见《论语·颜渊》。
❷《论语·雍也》。
❸《论语·宪问》。

❶ See "Yan Yuan," *Lunyu*.
❷ "Yongye," *Lunyu*.
❸ "Xianwen," *Lunyu*.

of speech, Confucius felt that Ran Yong was not necessarily humane, and why did he need eloquence anyway? He further stated that he did not know whether or not Zilu, Ran You and Gongxi Hua belonged to the class of those possessing the virtue of humaneness. And that famous politician Guan Zhong, despite the defects of lacking frugality and not knowing the rites, should still be considered as truly possessing the virtue of humaneness because of his political merit in aiding Duke Huan of Qi to "convene the feudal princes nine times but not utilize the force of arms." From this we may observe that the merit of "comforting the people" was a key factor. Of course, "humaneness" was not necessarily "broadly ministering" or "saving the masses," because these required a certain amount of material pre-conditions. Confucius felt that even such sages as Yao and Shun would not necessarily have been able to completely accomplish this, because they may have not possessed these preconditions. Therefore, what "humaneness" first of all indicated was an internal moral cultivation, the internal moral orientation associated with such qualities as "loving others" and "loyalty and reciprocity."

Finally, let's look at the relationship between "humaneness" and the cultivation of character. In order to seek "humaneness," it is necessary to engage in an internal process of moral cultivation, to complete an independent human character. Confucius felt that the achievement of an ideal character was reached by worthies and gentlemen after perfecting their moral virtues, and finally achieving the goals of perfecting sagacity and of "comforting the people." However, this requires that those in power "elevate the worthy and talented" before this is able to happen. As for those who cultivated the inner virtue of humaneness yet were unable to serve in office as officials, Confucius advocated that they assert their own individual spirits in order to form an independent character. Realistically, many *shi* of lofty morality were not utilized by those in power. So these men often had to form their own independent characters. They not only were able to serve the rulers, but also became the critics of the actual rulers, and thereby formed a class of *shi* with independent characters. During the course of the rise of the *shi*, Confucius played an important role; he decided the basic character of this social class. To Confucius, the ideal human character was one that was aware of its self-worth, and possessed the moral virtues of wisdom, humaneness, and bravery, like the saying, "The wise are not deluded, the humane do not worry, and the brave are not afraid." ❶ "Not deluded," "not worried," and "not afraid" precisely indicate asserting a strong spirit of self, and are manifestations of the spirit of an independent character that is not disturbed by the external

时，孔子认为冉雍未必仁，哪里需要有口才呢？又说：不知道子路、冉有、公西华是不是属于具有仁德的人。而著名的政治家管仲，虽然他有不节俭、不知礼仪的缺陷，但因为他有辅助齐桓公"九合诸侯，不以兵车"的政治功绩，孔子认为管仲是真正具有仁德的人。可见，"安百姓"的功绩是关键因素。当然，"仁"，并不一定是"博施"、"济众"，因为这需要有一定的物质条件。孔子认为，即使尧、舜这样的圣者也未必能够完全做到，就是因为尧、舜未必有这样的条件。因此，"仁"首先指的是内在的道德修养，是关于"爱人"、"忠恕"等内在的价值取向。

最后，"仁"与人格培养的关系。求"仁"就是要进行内在道德的修养，成就独立人格。孔子认为，理想人格的实现是贤人君子通过修己成德，最后达到成圣、"安百姓"的目的。但是，这需要执政者"举贤才"才能实现。对于内修仁德而没有能够从政为官的人，孔子则提倡挺立自我精神，以成就独立人格。现实中很多道德高洁之士往往不被执政者所用，这些人往往形成了独立的人格。他们既可以为统治者服务，也可能成为现实政治的批判者，从而形成具有独立人格的士的阶层。孔子在士的兴起过程中起到了重要的作用，他为士的阶层确定了基本品格。在孔子看来，理想的人格是具有自我意识的人格，具有智、仁、勇的品德，所谓"知（智）者不惑，仁者不忧，勇者不惧"❶。"不惑"、"不忧"、"不惧"正是指挺立自我精神，不受外在政治环境干扰的独立人格精神的表现。孔子说：

❶《论语·子罕》。

❶ "Zihan," *Lunyu.*

political environment. Confucius said, "You can kidnap the commander of the whole armies, but you cannot take away the will from an ordinary man." ❶ This means that an army may lose its commander, but you cannot force a man of ambition to abandon what he cherishes. What Confucius insisted on was the value of an independent will. Of course, to steadfastly maintain an independent will often require one to pay a high price. Confucius highly admired the boundless spirit of those men of lofty ideals who were not afraid of difficulties nor afraid of pressure. He said, "Only when fierce cold has come do you realize that the pines and cypresses have lost their leaves." ❷ He further said, "Men of lofty ideals do not injure their virtue of humaneness because they are poor or afraid of death; rather, they are bold in making sacrifices to complete their virtue of humaneness." ❸ From this we may observe that Confucius felt that the body of the humane person should be subject to moral rationality. He pointed out that the gentleman "worries over the Way, not over poverty," and should not take into consideration personal benefits; his only personal end should be his moral nature, that is, his "humaneness" and the "Way." It is evident that during the course of the formation and development of the class of *shi* in ancient China, Confucius endowed it with an independent character that was not influenced by one's environment and a sense of self-worth, and to a certain degree, it inherited the role of being the conscience of society and the standard of righteousness of the race. At the same time, the sense of responsibility of men of lofty ideals possessed strength of spirit that was awe-inspiring as manifested in the course of revolution by the people and the rise and fall of states. As for the transmission of culture and the race this spirit played an important role. And the kind of character mentioned above was none other than the manifestation of the virtue of humaneness.

Confucius felt that the virtue of humaneness was the highest form of personal moral conduct possessed by the ancient worthies. Boyi and Shuqi both were humble and yielding, and not willing to become the lords of the state of Guzhu, so they fled to a neighboring state. Ultimately they died of hunger, having no qualms. They were men of humaneness. Yet this does not imply that the humane are not social creatures. Actually, what Confucius taught about "humaneness" was the need to form an integrated human character, not to completely deny the natural desire of humans. What Confucius said about "overcoming the self and returning to the rites" means to use the "rites" to overcome the "self." And the "rites" determine one's position in the midst of social relations and social pecking order. They do not imply the

"三军可夺帅也，匹夫不可夺志也。" ❶意思是说，一国的军队可以失去主帅，但却不能强迫志士放弃主张。孔子坚持的是独立意志的可贵。当然，坚守独立意志，往往需要付出较大的代价，孔子对那些不畏困难，不惧压力的志士仁人的浩然正气十分赞叹，他说："严寒时节，才知道松柏最后凋叶。" ❷又说："志士仁人，不是贪生怕死而损害仁德，而是勇于牺牲来成全仁德。" ❸ 可以看出，孔子认为仁人的身体应该服从于道德理性。他提出，君子"忧道不忧贫"，不应该考虑个人得失，而应该以德性，也就是"仁"与"道"为自我的唯一归宿。可见，在中国古代士阶层的形成与发展过程中，孔子赋予了其不受环境影响的独立人格和自我意识，并在某种程度上承载着社会的良知，民族的正义。同时，志士仁人所具有的担当意识，在民族大义、国家兴亡之时具有令人震慑的精神力量，对于文化的传承、民族的传衍（yǎn）产生了重要的作用。而这种人格，就是仁德的体现。

　　孔子认为，仁德是古代贤士们具有的最高道德操守，伯夷、叔齐两人互相推让，不肯做孤竹国的国君而逃到国外，最终饿死而无怨，他们是仁德之人。但这并不意味着仁人不食人间烟火，其实孔子所说的"仁"，是要树立一个完整的人格，而并不是完全否认人的自然欲求。孔子讲"克己复礼为仁"，是说用"礼"来战胜"己"，而"礼"是从社会关系、社会秩序中确定人的地位，并不意味着就是泯灭人的真情实感。对此，

❶《论语·子罕》。
❷ 见《论语·子罕》。
❸ 见《论语·卫灵公》。

❶ "Zihan," *Lunyu*.
❷ See "Zihan," *Lunyu*.
❸ See "Weilinggong," *Lunyu*.

elimination of true personal feelings. Concerning this, the *Analects* includes the following record: Confucius' student Yuan Xian asked, "As for striving to be better than others, boastfulness, resentment and desires— if these are eliminated, can one return to humaneness?" This means that if these four kinds of negative emotions are not manifested, is such a person to be considered humane? Confucius responded, "We may term such an individual very commendable indeed, but if you call him humane, I do not know about that." ❶ Although Confucius said he did not know whether such an individual was humane or not, actually this was merely a tactful way to say that this individual was not humane. Mr. Feng Youlan felt that "humaneness" meant that one had to accomplish what is known as "extending to the other person," and simultaneously needed to "overcome the self" ; that is, to learn to control oneself and to be able to extend sympathetic understanding to others. He explained this by using the later debate between Mencius and King Xuan of Qi concerning "being fond of sex and commodities" : "If King Xuan of Qi understands that his subjects are ' fond of sex and commodities' because of his own feelings regarding them, and then adopts measures to help them to satisfy these feelings, this then is the definition of 'a humane government,' 'extending oneself,' and 'overcoming the self.' " Therefore, Mr. Feng Youlan feels that what the *Doctrine of the Mean* teaches concerning "to be humane is to be human," precisely embodies all of the character elements contained in Confucius' expression of "humaneness." ❷ It is precisely because seeking "humaneness" is the focal point that men establish themselves and accomplish things. To seek humaneness is to realize a perfect character. Therefore Confucius said that if a person lacks the virtue of humaneness, how can he handle the ritual system? If he is human but not humane, then what does he have to do with music? ❸

Second is about views regarding the "rites." In the main Confucius discussed the essence of "ritual" and its relationship with "humaneness."

First of all, let's discuss the essence of "ritual." The "rites" discussed by Confucius were a formalized process devised by the rulers desiring to establish a relationship with the spirits. By extending them throughout each level of society, they became important means to differentiate between members of society. Confucius said concerning this, "I have heard that the most important foundation of the lives of the people is ritual. Without ritual it is impossible to sacrifice to either heavenly spirits or earthly spirits; without ritual one cannot

《论语》中有这样的记载，孔子的学生原宪问："克、伐、怨、欲不行焉，可以归仁矣。"意思是说，好胜、自夸、怨恨和欲望四种感情都没有表现过，可以说是仁人了吧？孔子回答说："可以说是难能可贵了，但是，如果说是仁人，那我就不知道了。"❶虽然孔子说不知道是否是仁，其实委婉地表明了这并不是仁。冯友兰先生认为，"仁"要做到的是"推己及人"，同时还要"克己"，就是克制自己而能够推己及人。他举了后来孟子和齐宣王关于"好色"、"好货"的辩论来说明，说："如果齐宣王因他自己'好色'、'好货'，由此而认识他的百姓也都'好色'、'好货'，并且施行一种措施，使他们都能满足他们的'好色'、'好货'，这就是'仁政'，这是'推己'，也就是'克己'。"所以，冯友兰先生认为，《中庸》中所说的"仁者，人也"正体现了孔子"仁"所要表现的完全人格的内涵。❷正因为求"仁"是人们立身行事的基本点，求"仁"是要实现完全的人格，所以孔子说，人如果没有仁德，怎样来对待礼仪制度呢？人如果没有仁德，怎样来对待音乐呢？❸

二、关于"礼"。孔子主要讨论了"礼"的本质、"礼"与"仁"的关系。

首先，"礼"的本质。孔子所说的"礼"是因统治者要与神灵建立关系而制定的形式化的程序，并延伸到社会的各阶层，成为区分社会成员的重要形式。对此，孔子说："我听说过百姓生存的根据，礼最为重要。没有礼就无法分别祭祀天神祇（qí），没有礼就不能区别君臣、上下、长幼，没有礼就无法区

❶ 见《论语·宪问》。
❷ 见《中国哲学史新编》第四章《前期儒家思想的形成——孔丘对于古代精神生活的反思》。
❸ 《论语·八佾》："人而不仁，如礼何？人而不仁，如乐何？"

❶ See "Xianwen," *Lunyu*.
❷ See Chapter Four, "The Formation of the Early Period of Confucianism—Confucius' Reflections on the Spiritual Life of Ancient China," in *The History of Chinese Philosophy*, new ed.
❸ "Baiyi," *Lunyu*.

distinguish between lords and ministers, upper and lower, young and old. Without ritual then one cannot distinguish between such familial relations, near and far, as men and women, fathers and sons, and older and younger brothers." ❶ Therefore, ritual is the system and the norm of the patriarchal clan system and the various ranks throughout society, and it is the most important thing in social and political life. The foundation and essence of "ritual," as Confucius discussed it, is "righteousness." Confucius said, "The gentleman takes righteousness as his foundation, he relies on ritual to act, expresses himself in humble language, and completes things through sincerity. If this is the case, then he truly is a gentleman!" ❷ This is to say that "ritual" is the manifestation of "righteousness," and that "righteousness" is the basis of "ritual" and its essence. Confucius does not base himself on an external "heaven" but instead on the internal "righteousness" possessed by man, that is to say he follows the principle of what is suitable to do. Confucius' student Youzi once said, "The application of ritual lies in harmony." ❸ The utility of the ritual then is valuable in how it promotes harmony; from this we may observe that ritual is used to adjust human relations.

Since the essence of "ritual" is "righteousness," that is to say, suitability and appropriateness being the standards, "centrality" then is a sphere related to "ritual." Confucius said, "Oh ritual! Now ritual is what is used to control centrality." ❹ This means that: Oh ritual, it decides what is central. It is evident that "ritual" is the internal regulatory mechanism of the "centrality." Confucius said, "Hold onto the two edges, but apply the centrality to the people." ❺ This means to grasp two outer edges to apply what is in between to the people; this "centrality" is then "ritual." Well then, what is the content of the "centrality" ? First, "centrality" indicates "nothing surpassing and nothing but reaches," which is to say that nothing goes beyond it and everything reaches it. The phrase "surpassing it and not reaching" means going beyond it equals to not reaching it; neither element is commensurate with the principle of the "centrality." When Zigong asked Confucius who was a little better, Zizhang or Zixia, Confucius replied, "Zizhang is somewhat excessive; Zixia is somewhat under reaching." Zigong asked, "Then is Zizhang somewhat better?" Confucius answered, saying, "Both excessive and under reaching are equally bad." ❻ Second, what Confucius meant by "centrality" changed according to

别男女、父子、兄弟等家庭、亲戚的亲疏远近。"❶因此，礼是宗法等级社会的制度、规范，礼是社会政治生活中最重要的东西。孔子所论的"礼"的根据与本质是"义"。孔子说："君子以义为本，依礼来实行，用谦逊的言语来表现，以诚信来完成。如果这样，就真是个君子啊！"❷这就是说"礼"是"义"的表现，"义"是"礼"之本、"礼"之质。孔子不以外在的"天"，而是以人所具有的"义"，也就是适宜为原则。孔子的学生有子说过："礼之用，和为贵。"❸礼的作用贵在和谐，可见，礼是用来调节人际关系的。

　　"礼"既然以"义"为本质，也就是以适宜、适中为准则，那么，"中"也是与"礼"相关联的范畴。孔子说："礼乎礼！夫礼所以制中也。"❹意思是：礼啊礼，礼决定中。可见，"礼"是"中"所具有的内在规定性。孔子说："执其两端，用其中于民。"❺就是把握两端，对百姓用两端之"中"，这个"中"就是"礼"。那么，"中"有哪些含义呢？第一，"中"是指"无过无不及"，也就是说既没有超过，也没有达不到；"过犹不及"，也就是超过与达不到一样，都不符合"中"的原则。当子贡问子张与子夏谁更好一些时，孔子说："子张有些过分，子夏有些达不到。"子贡就说："那么是不是子张好一些？"孔子回答说："过分与达不到一样不好。"❻第二，孔子

❶ 见《礼记·哀公问》。
❷ 见《论语·卫灵公》。
❸《论语·学而》。
❹《礼记·仲尼燕居》。
❺《礼记·中庸》。
❻ 见《论语·先进》。

❶ See "Aigongwen," *Liji*.
❷ See "Weilinggong," *Lunyu*.
❸ "Xue' er," *Lunyu*.
❹ "Zhongni Yanju," *Liji*.
❺ "Zhongyong," *Liji*.
❻ See "Xianjin," *Lunyu*.

when he discussed it; this is what he meant by saying "The gentleman uses the centrality according to the time." Connected to this is the "ritual" that determines the "centrality" ; in the same way it can change according to the time. When Confucius mentioned "return to ritual," he was targeting the contemporary phenomena of "the rites crumbled and music was destroyed," and was not just heedlessly following the Zhou system of ritual and restoring it for no reason. "Ritual" itself possessed the principle of "using the centrality according to the time," and can also change according to the time. Of course, during the course of change, one must maintain one's value system and ideals. Just as Confucius said, "A hempen cap, this is according to ritual. Now they use black gauze, which is more frugal. I follow the general practice. To bow before ascending is according to ritual. But now they bow on top of the stairs, which is arrogant. Although I go against the crowd, I follow the practice of bowing below." ❶ The type of "rituals" mentioned here are all concrete ceremonies; they were based on Zhou practice but some accommodations had been made. The above line then means that the cap to be used in ritual ceremony should be knit out of hemp, this is in keeping with the traditional rite. But nowadays, everyone uses silk, which is more economical; I agree with the modern practice. When a minister sees his lord, he should first make a bow below the hall, then ascend and make another bow; this is in keeping with traditional ritual etiquette. But now everyone dispenses with the bow below the hall, and only makes the bow in the hall. It is an arrogant practice. Although I go against the modern practice, I still advocate the necessity of bowing below the hall. Confucius felt that "changes" or "accommodations" in the "rites" depended on whether or not they meshed with the moral principles of respectfulness or frugality. Moreover, Confucius linked up "centrality" with "commonality." He said, "The mean (centrality together with commonality) is the highest form of virtue, but the people have lacked it for a long time." ❷ What is meant by "commonality" is "what is common." "Commonality" is the same with "centrality" ; both are universal truths and laws that exist in the real world. "Ritual," then, is the manifestation of these laws and set truths. "Ritual" also changes and promotes change following the times. Ritual not only exerts a restraining effect, but also simultaneously harmonizes various relationships that occur with change in reality over time.

　　Next is the relationship between "ritual" and "humaneness." "Ritual" is an important topic in the *Analects*, second only to "humaneness." In order to understand the position of "ritual" in the thought of Confucius, it is necessary to grasp the relationship between "ritual" and "humaneness." Concerning this,

所说的"中"是因时而改变的,这就是孔子说的君子"时中"。与此相联系,决定"中"的"礼"同样可以因时而变。孔子所说的"复礼"是孔子针对当时"礼崩乐坏"现象而发的,并不是无原则地遵守周礼,恢复周礼。"礼"也具有"时中"的原则,也可以因时而变,当然在变的过程中还坚持着自己的价值理念。如孔子说:"麻冕,礼也。今也纯,俭,吾从众。拜下,礼也。今拜乎上,泰也。虽违众,吾从下。"❶ 这里的"礼",都是具体的礼仪,这个礼仪,既本于周礼,又有变通。这句话的意思是说,礼帽用麻料来织,这是合于传统的礼的;今天大家都用丝料,这样省俭些,我同意大家的做法。臣见君,先在堂下磕头,然后升堂又磕头,这是合于传统的礼的。今天大家都免除了堂下的磕头,只在升堂后磕头,这是傲慢的表现。虽然违反大家的做法,我仍然主张要先在堂下磕头。孔子认为"礼"的"变"与"不变"在于是否符合恭、俭的道德原则。孔子还将"中"与"庸"联系起来,他说:"中庸是最高的道德,民众缺乏它很久了。"❷ 所谓"庸",就是"平常"的意思。"庸"与"中"一样,都是现实世界存在着的普遍道理与规律,而"礼"就是这种规律与定理的表现。"礼"也是可以随着时代的改变而发生变化的。礼既有制约的功能,同时,还可以根据现实的变化来调节社会的种种关系。

其次,"礼"与"仁"的关系。"礼"是《论语》中仅次于"仁"的一个重要范畴。要了解"礼"在孔子思想体系中的地位,就必须理清"礼"与"仁"的关系。对此,《论语》中看

❶《论语·子罕》。
❷ 见《论语·雍也》。

❶ "Zihan," *Lunyu*.
❷ See "Yongye," *Lunyu*.

the *Analects* seem to make a circular argument. For instance, on the one hand Confucius uses "ritual" to determine "humaneness," stating, "Overcoming the self and returning the ritual is humaneness." ❶ On the other hand, he uses "humaneness" to determine "ritual," saying "How can one without humaneness perform ritual?" According to the theory of Mr. Feng Youlan, this is because Confucius wanted to build a perfect human character. He said

> this is due to Confucius' thinking including a perfect moral quality, that of the unity of "humaneness" and "ritual." But "humaneness" and "ritual" are mutually contradictory. "Humaneness" is something that belongs to personal liberty; while "ritual" is something pertaining to societal restraints. "Humaneness" is something that belongs to a natural gift, while "ritual" is something pertaining to man-made artistry.... If "ritual" does not include any truly emotional content, it is an empty framework. Strictly speaking, it cannot turn into "humaneness." But true emotions, without the restraint of "ritual," also strictly speaking, cannot turn into "humaneness" either. Therefore, true "ritual" must include "humaneness," and perfect "humaneness" must include "ritual." They are two opposites that interpenetrate each other, and so form a perfect moral quality, the unity of "ritual" and "humaneness." A perfect human character is the manifestation of just such a unity. ❷

At the same time, the relationship between ritual and humaneness is manifested in the aspect of politics. When Duke Ai of Lu asked Confucius about ritual, Confucius said, "Anciently in enacting government, it was most important to love the people. To manifest this, the most important thing was ritual. And to manifest ritual, the most important thing was respect." ❸ This means that, with regard to government, humaneness was the foundation, and ritual was the most important form for manifesting it. Viewed from this point of view, "humaneness" and "ritual" reflected the relationship between "culture" and "nature" that Confucius spoke of. Therefore, "When culture and nature are in harmony, one can be a gentleman." This relationship is also useful in understanding the relationship between "humaneness" and "ritual."

似有循环论证。如，一方面，孔子用"礼"来规定"仁"，说："克己复礼为仁"，另一方面，又以"仁"来规定"礼"，说："人而不仁如礼何？"❶根据冯友兰先生的说法，这是由于孔子要建立一个完全的人格。他说：

> 这是因为在他（孔子）的思想中，一个完全的道德品质，是"仁"和"礼"的统一。"仁"和"礼"是互相矛盾的。"仁"是属于个人的自由这一方面的东西；"礼"是属于社会的制裁这一方面的东西。"仁"是属于自然的礼物这一方面的东西；"礼"是属于人为的艺术这一方面的东西。……没有真情实感为内容的"礼"，就是一个空架子，严格地说，就不成其为"礼"。没有礼的节制的真情实感，严格地说，也不成其为"仁"。所以真正的"礼"必包含有"仁"；完全的"仁"也必包含有"礼"。这就是两个对立面的互相渗透。所以一个完全的道德品质，就是"礼"和"仁"的统一。一个完全的人格，就是这个统一的体现。❷

同时，仁与礼的关系还体现在政治方面。当鲁哀公向孔子问礼时，孔子说："古代为政，爱人最重要；用来表现爱人的，礼最重要；用来表现礼的，敬最重要。"❸这是说，在政治方面，仁为根本，礼是体现仁的最重要的形式。从这个意义上说，"仁"与"礼"就是孔子所说的"文"与"质"的关系，因此，"文质彬彬，然后君子"，也适用于对"仁"与"礼"关系的理解。

❶《论语·八佾》。
❷《中国哲学史新编》第四章《前期儒家思想的形成——孔丘对于古代精神生活的反思》。
❸ 见《礼记·哀公问》。

❶ " Bayi," *Lunyu*.
❷ Chapter Four, " The Formation of the Early Period of Confucianism—Confucius' Reflections on the Spiritual Life of Ancient China," in the *History of Chinese Philosophy*, new ed.
❸ See " Aigongwen," *Liji*.

However, when "ritual," as the outward form of human character, is manifested outwardly in society, and after it is manifested in the social structure and set into specific forms, "ritual" then possesses a distinctive characteristic that differentiates it from "humaneness," which is the main manifestation of personal inward morality. "Ritual" also possesses a relative independence. Therefore, "ritual" possesses a content including such aspects based on culture as the social system, standards of conduct, and ceremonial rites. What Confucius mentioned as the "rites" of the "Three Dynasties" in the main referred to the system of rites. From Confucius' point of view, it was hard to reconstruct or verify the rites of the Xia and Yin dynasties since historical records were lacking; therefore Confucius especially esteemed the rites of Zhou. He said, "The ritual system of the Zhou Dynasty was based on the Xia and Yin, and was rich and varied. I follow the rites of the Zhou." ❶ Confucius felt that "ritual" at the level of the system can be changed. He said, "Yin followed the rites of Xia, and then what was changed may be known." ❷ "Changed" means what was added or subtracted, and also means what was inherited and what was reformed. But Confucius opposed the usurping, who turned against ritual propriety; this substantially demonstrates that Confucius longed for social stability in order to prevent a scenario of chaos in the political order. "Ritual" at the level of the system does not necessarily mesh with the "humaneness" that reveals personal morality. For instance, Confucius felt that Guan Zhong was a "humane" person, but Guan Zhong did not know "ritual." When someone asked Confucius whether Guan Zhong knew "ritual," Confucius said, "A screen gate was erected in the front of the palace of the lord of the state, Guan Zhong also erected a screen gate; when the lord of the state hosted a banquet to receive foreign heads of state, he set up a stand for the liquor goblets; Guan Zhong also had the same type of stand. So if you say that Guan Zhong knows ritual, then who does not know ritual?" ❸ What Guan Zhong contravened was the rites of Zhou. When "humaneness" and "ritual" came into conflict, Confucius stood on the side of "humaneness." Although Guan Zhong "did not know ritual," and "was not frugal," still Confucius fully affirmed Guan Zhong's merit. He said, "If it were not for Guan Zhong, we would still be letting our hair hang loose, and buttoning our coats on the left." ❹ This means that they would have declined into a culturally backwards people.

　　然而，当作为人格的表现形式的"礼"外化于社会，并体现在社会制度与礼仪形式的层面之后，"礼"便具有了与主要体现个人内在德性的"仁"相区别的特征，并具有了相对独立性。因此，"礼"还有以文化为核心要素的包括社会制度、行为规范、礼节仪式等多方面的内容，孔子所说的"三代"之"礼"，就主要是从制度层面而言的。在孔子看来，夏、殷之礼因文献缺失，已难以考求，所以孔子特别重视周礼，他说："周朝的礼仪制度是按夏商两代制定的，丰富多彩。我遵循周朝的礼仪。"❶孔子认为制度层面的"礼"是可以改变的，他说"殷因于夏礼，所损益可知也"❷，"损益"就是增减，也就是既有继承又有变革。但孔子反对违背礼仪的"僭（jiàn）越"，这实质表示了孔子期望社会安宁，以防出现政治秩序混乱的局面。制度层面的"礼"，未必与表示个人德性的"仁"在个人那里得到统一。如，孔子认为管仲是"仁"者，但管仲并不知"礼"。当有人问孔子管仲是否知礼时，孔子说："国君宫殿门前，立了一个塞门，管仲也立个塞门；国君设宴招待外国的君主，在堂上有放置酒杯的器具，管仲也有这样的器具。如果说他懂礼节，那谁不懂得礼节呢？"❸管仲所违反的，正是周礼。当"仁"与"礼"发生矛盾时，孔子更重视"仁"。虽然管仲"不知礼"，"不俭"，但是，孔子还是充分肯定了管仲的功绩，他说："假若没有管仲，我们都还披散着头发，穿着衣襟向左边开的衣服。"❹也就是说可能沦落为落后的民族。

❶ 见《论语·八佾》。
❷《论语·为政》。
❸ 见《论语·八佾》。
❹ 见《论语·宪问》。

❶ See "Bayi," *Lunyu*.
❷ "Weizheng," *Lunyu*.
❸ See "Bayi," *Lunyu*.
❹ See "Xianwen," *Lunyu*.

Viewed from this point of view, Confucius greatly esteemed Guan Zhong. Therefore, in comparing "humaneness" and "ritual," "humaneness" was more foundational, and more important. Of course, compared with the relative independence of "ritual," the unity between "humaneness" and "ritual" is even more foundational. With regard to this, Mr. Kuang Yaming keenly analyzed this from the angles of society and ethics:

> Ritual is the system and the norm of the patriarchal clan system and the various ranks throughout society; it stresses the order of high and low, old and young, and embodies the distinctions and oppositions of the different statuses of people. According to its original meaning, humaneness is a kind of humanistic thought, stressing love, understanding, concern, and tolerance among people; it also stresses the stability and elevation of the material lives of the great mass of the people, etc. Viewed from the aspect of society and the government, if only ritual were present but no humaneness, this would increase the juxtaposition of opposites, and lead to the intensification of contradictions and the creation of crises throughout society. But if only humaneness were present, but no ritual, this would produce undifferentiated love, and blur the distinctions between high and low, honored and base. Confucius hoped that these two polarities would not emerge....
>
> Viewed from the aspect of Confucius' ethics, ritual is the standard of human conduct, and embodies the social restraints society imposes on the individual. On the other hand, humaneness is the essential quality of a person; it is the internal self-awareness of personal self-cultivation and of loving others. With only external constraints but no internal awareness, then human conduct would be completely the result of compulsion, and would lose what it is that makes one human. But with only internal self-awareness and without external restraints, then each would act according to his own lights, and the order of honored and base, high and low would not be possible to be maintained. Therefore, the external and the internal, ritual and humaneness, must all be unified. One must enact humaneness according to the standards of ritual, and to use humaneness to become self-aware in enacting ritual. ❶

Mr. Feng Youlan and Mr. Kuang Yaming both independently and minutely

由此可见，孔子对于管仲是十分尊敬的。因此，"仁"与"礼"相比，"仁"更为本质、更为重要。当然，与"礼"的相对独立性相比，"仁"与"礼"的统一性更为本质，对此，匡亚明先生从社会、伦理的角度进行了精要的分析：

> 礼是宗法等级社会的制度、规范，它强调的是尊卑长幼之序，是具有不同名分的人之间的区别与对立。仁按其本义是一种人道主义思想，强调人们之间的仁爱、谅解、关怀、容忍，也强调广大人民物质生活的安定和提高等等。从社会政治方面看，如果只有礼而没有仁，那就会加深对立，导致矛盾激化，造成社会危机。如果只有仁而没有礼，就会产生没有差等的仁爱，以致模糊上下尊卑的界限。这两极都是孔子所不希望出现的。……

> 从孔子伦理学角度去看，礼是人们的行为准则，体现了社会对人的外在约束；仁则是人的本质，是修己、爱人的内在自觉性。只有外在约束而无内在自觉，则人的行为完全成为强制的结果，失去人之所以为人的特点；只有内在自觉而无外在约束，则人人按自己标准行事，不能保持尊卑上下的秩序。因此外与内、礼与仁必须统一起来。以礼的准则行仁，以仁的自觉复礼。❶

冯友兰先生与匡亚明先生分别从完全人格的构成和伦理、

❶《孔子评传》第四章《仁的人生哲学思想》。

❶ Chapter Four, "The Philosophical Thought of Human Life According to Humaneness," in *Critical Biography of Confucius*.

investigated the relationship between the two important realms of the development of the ethics of a perfect human character plus the social level of "humaneness" together with "ritual." They both indicated that "humaneness" and "ritual" enjoyed the inner and outer relationship of a single organic entity. "Humaneness" and "ritual" created the foundation of Confucius' views on ethics, society, politics, and education, even religion. "Overcome the self and return to ritual" concisely manifested the fundamental elements and inner relationships of Confucius' thought.

社会的层面对"仁"与"礼"这两个最为重要的范畴之间的关系进行了精辟的分析，都指出了"仁"与"礼"是一体共生的表里关系。"仁"与"礼"构成了孔子伦理、社会、政治、教育乃至宗教观念的基础。"克己复礼为仁"，简明地表现了孔子思想的基本元素及其内在联系。

《论语》书影

Picture of the *Analects*

八 "有教无类"——孔子的教育思想

Chapter Ⅷ " Teaching Without Regard to Class" : Confucius' Educational Thought

Most of Confucius' life was spent in educating students; his educational thought is the most vital portion of all his thought. Confucius' educational theory was rich in content, involving such aspects as the target of education, the purpose of education, the content of education, and the methodology of education, etc. "Teaching without regard to class" is the educational viewpoint that education should be fair, and comprehensive in elevating the quality of men without regard to social class or regional derivation. It may be termed the overall guiding principle and fundamental characteristic of Confucius' educational thought.

First of all, concerning the target of education, Confucius proposed "teaching without regard to class." ❶ This is the principle that one's position, honored or base, does not impact education. Confucius let the sons of members of each level of society receive an opportunity for education; this inaugurated the universal availability of culture and education. During the Yin and Zhou periods only the sons of the aristocracy had the right to receive education. During the Spring and Autumn Period, cultural education underwent some changes; this is "When the Son of Heaven lost his officers, learning occurred among the four barbarians." ❷ This means that after state-run schools began to decline, private schools among the people began to flourish. Culture transferred from officialdom and the capital to the people and border regions. During this transitional process, Confucius played an important role; he started a private school, accepted students on a broad basis, and became the founder of private schools in our nation. Confucius' promotion of the principle of "teaching without regard to class" destroyed the aristocratic monopoly on cultural education, allowing commoners to enjoy the right to education; this is precisely a manifestation of the spirit of love. This principle became freshly manifested in the practical application of his educational program. Confucius accepted students without regard to regional derivation or social status, only requiring that they give some dried meat as a sign of respect, they then would be accepted. Among the 77 students (in the main, 35), recorded in "Biographies of Confucius' Disciples," in the *Reocords of the Grand Historian*, as for their backgrounds, there was Yan Hui who lived on a dilapidated old lane, Ran Yong, whose father was considered lowly, and Zilu, who was from the country. There was also Duanmu Ci, who was "fond of commodities" (doing business) and whose family owned a thousand catties of gold, and the teacher of Marquise Wen of Wei, Bu Shang. As for regional derivation, Yan Hui, Ran Qiu, Zai Yu, Fan Xu, et al. were from either Qi or Lu; Bu Shang and Duanmu Ci were from Wei, Sima Geng was from Song,

　　孔子一生大部分时间是在教育学生中度过的，教育思想也是孔子思想中最具生命力的部分。孔子的教育学说具有丰富的内容，涉及教育对象、教学目的、教学内容、教学方法等不同的方面，"有教无类"就是不分阶层、不分地域，全面提升人的素质的平等教育观念，堪称孔子教育思想的总纲领和基本特色。

　　首先，关于教育对象，孔子提出"有教无类"❶，也就是教育不受贵贱身份影响的原则。孔子让各阶层的子弟有接受教育的机会，实开文化、教育普及的先河。殷周时期只有贵族子弟才有接受教育的权利，春秋时期，文化教育出现了一些新的变化，这就是"天子失官，学在四夷"❷，也就是官办学校已日益衰落，民间的私学已逐渐兴起，文化从官府以及京城向民间与边远地区转移，在这一风气转变的过程中，孔子起到了重要的作用。孔子兴办私学，广收门徒，成为我国兴办私学的创始人。孔子提出的"有教无类"的原则，打破了贵族垄断文化教育的局面，使平民子弟享有受教育的权利，正是其仁爱精神的体现。这个原则在其教学实践中得到了鲜明的体现，孔子招收学生不分地域、尊卑，只要给一些干肉，以示尊敬，就可以入门。在《史记·仲尼弟子列传》所记载的七十七人（主要是三十五人）中，就出身而言，有身居陋巷的颜回，有其父为"贱人"的冉雍，有"野人"出身的子路，还有善于"货殖"（做买卖），家有千金的端木赐，有魏文侯的老师卜商。就地域而言，颜回、冉求、宰予、樊须等人为齐鲁人，卜商、端木赐为卫人，司马耕为宋人，公良孺为陈人，言偃为吴人，叔仲会

❶《论语·卫灵公第十五》。
❷《左传·昭公十七年》。

❶ "Weilinggong the 15th," *Lunyu*.
❷ "Zhaogong 17th year," *Zuozhuan*.

Gongliang Ru was from Chen, Yan Yan was from Wu, Shuzhong Hui was from Jin, Qin Zu was from Qin, and Gongsun Long was from Chu. It is evident that Confucius' disciples came from both high and low backgrounds, and the state affiliations were all different. As for Confucius' practice of accepting students regardless of background or state affiliation, it was hard for some people to understand. According to historical accounts, Nanguo Huizi once asked Zigong, "Why does Confucius accept such a mixed bag of students?" Zigong replied, "On the side of a good physician are many sick persons, and next to a wood straightening tool are many pieces of crooked wood; therefore, the students accepted by Confucius are of a mixed bag." ❶

Next is regarding the purpose of education. Confucius' views on equal and universal education sought to comprehensively develop individual talent in order to achieve the elevation of the morals of the entire society. Confucius' views on education and individual talent were an extension of his views on politics as being "politics through virtue." With regard to the relationship between virtue and talent, Confucius advocated virtue as a priority; he felt that a person must have a loyal, trustworthy, and all-encompassing kind of moral character, and afterwards could come the demand for wisdom and ability. The basic ideal of Confucius' educational thought was to teach others to perfect their morality, which means the cultivation of their characters. The mere conveyance of knowledge was not the first duty in Confucius' educational thought. For instance, Confucius regarded Yan Hui as loving learning, but this did not mean that Yan Hui was erudite, rather that Yan Hui "would not get mad at a person just because he was mad at someone else or make a double fault." ❷ This meant that he would not vent himself at someone else's expense, nor commit the same error twice. It is obvious that what Confucius meant by "loving learning" meant the improvement of morals; therefore, Confucius' educational thought actually included the education of knowledge and of ethics, but moral cultivation was the first demand.

Although the purpose of Confucius' moral education was to teach how to become a sage, nevertheless in reality a sage who was born knowing the Way hardly ever existed. To him, a sage actually referred to those outstanding men in history who had already passed away, such as Yu, Tang, Wen, Wu, and the Duke of Zhou. What existed in reality were merely those "gentlemen" who knew the Way through learning it. Once he said that he had never seen a sage; what he had seen were merely gentlemen. This was all. Therefore, becoming a sage was merely the ideal goal of Confucius' educational program, while developing a "gentleman" of perfect character was the realistic goal of Confucius' educational program. Well, just what characteristics did a

为晋人，秦祖为秦人，公孙龙为楚人。可见，孔门弟子身份贵贱有别，出生国籍各有不同。对于孔子不分尊卑和国籍招收门徒的做法，一些人很不理解。据记载，南郭惠子曾问子贡说："孔子招收的门徒为什么这样杂啊？"子贡说："好的医生身旁多病人，栝（一种矫正竹木弯曲的工具）旁边多弯曲的木料，因此，孔子招收的门徒也比较杂。"❶

其次，关于教学目的。孔子平等、普及的教育观要求全面培养人才，以实现全社会的道德升华，孔子的教育观、人才观是他为政以德的政治观念的延伸。在德、才关系上，孔子主张以德为先，他认为人首先要具有忠信厚重的品德，然后才是对智能方面的要求。孔子教育思想的基本理念是教人成德，也就是人格的修养。知识传授并不是孔子教育思想的第一要务，如，孔子认为颜回好学，并不是指颜回博学多识，而是颜回"不迁怒，不贰过"❷，也就是不拿别人出气，不再犯同样的过失。显然孔子所说的"好学"是指道德的进步，因此，孔子的教育思想其实包含了知识教育与伦理教育的双重内容，而以道德修养为第一要义。

孔子的道德教育虽然以教人成圣为目的，但现实中生而知之的圣人在孔子看来几乎是不存在的，他眼中的圣人实际上仅是指历史上已故的杰出人物，如禹、汤、文、武、周公等人，现实中存在的仅是学而知之的"君子"。他曾经说过，圣人我没有见过，见到过的是君子，这就可以了。因此，成圣，仅是孔子教育的理想目标，而培养人格完美的"君子"才是孔子教学的现实目标。那么孔子所说的"君子"有哪些特征呢？孔子

❶ 见《荀子·法行》。
❷ 《论语·雍也》。

❶ See "Faxing," *Xunzi*.
❷ "Yongye," *Lunyu*.

so-called "gentleman" possess? Confucius felt that a "gentleman" was a man who had received a fine education and who possessed moral conduct in various forms. The most fundamental characteristic of a "gentleman" was to possess the virtue of humaneness; Confucius felt that if one abandoned humaneness, one could not achieve the fame of being known as a gentleman, for a gentleman never for an instance contravened the virtue of humaneness. Of course, as the highest moral standard, no gentleman ever possessed all the elements of "humaneness"; still, the gentleman was moving towards humaneness. This is just like Confucius said, "There are gentlemen who are not humane, but there has never been a petty person who was humane." ❶ In addition to this, a "gentleman" also incorporated the moral conduct of faithful performance of the rites, was humble in speech, restrained and not contentious, gregarious and not partial. Therefore, as a model of the character promoted by Confucius, the gentleman was not an isolated entity but was an individual who fully participated in all the relationships associated with the "rites." Developing and molding the character of a "gentleman" was the purpose of Confucius in educating his disciples. Achieving virtue then was the primary condition for developing a gentleman.

　　Confucius' views on education are comprehensive and systematic. Confucius felt that a "gentleman" should moreover embody the concrete manifestations of the virtue of humaneness—wisdom, bravery, and the like. Although Confucius humbly stated that he himself still did not possess these aspects of moral behavior, nevertheless Zigong felt that Confucius was, in fact, the model of the gentlemanly qualities of "humaneness," "wisdom," and "bravery." Among them the virtue of "wisdom" included gaining knowledge through study. Therefore, Confucius' teachings on perfecting virtue actually implied the integration of education on the virtue of humaneness with education for knowledge. Confucius felt that one who loves virtue but does not love learning has the character of an imperfect person, saying, "One who loves virtue but does not love learning has the defect of ignorance; one who loves wisdom but does not love learning has the defect of dissipation; one who loves sincerity yet does not love learning has the defect of ultimately harming oneself; one who loves straightforwardness yet does not love learning has the defect of using sharp language that harms others; one who loves bravery yet does not love learning has the defect of being rebellious; one who loves rigidity yet does not love learning has the defect of being arrogant." ❷ Confucius himself "at age 15 set his resolve on learning," ❸ ultimately acquiring the character of a sage. Because of Confucius' own life experiences, he

认为的"君子"，是受到良好教育，具备多种德行的人。"君子"最根本的特征是具有仁德，孔子认为如果抛弃了仁德，不能成就君子的美名，君子是没有片刻违背仁德的。当然，作为最高的道德标准，君子也未必完全具备"仁"的所有内涵，但君子一定是向往仁德的，即孔子所说："有君子而不仁的，但是没有小人而仁的。"❶此外，"君子"还具有信守义礼、出言谦虚、矜持而不争、合群而不结党等德行。因此，作为孔子所提倡的典范人格——君子，并不是孤立的个体，而是与他人一起参与到"礼"的关系中的个人。培养与塑造"君子"人格，是孔子教育弟子的目的，成德则是培养君子的首要条件。

孔子的教育观念是全面系统的，孔子认为，"君子"还应体现仁德的具体表现——智、勇等等。孔子虽然自谦地说自己尚不具备这些德行，但子贡认为孔子就是具备了"仁"、"智"、"勇"的"君子"的典范。其中"智"德包含了学习知识的内容，因此，孔子的成德之教其实就含有仁德教育与知识教育相结合的意味。孔子认为，好德而不好学是不完善的人格，说："好仁德而不好学，其流弊是愚昧；好智慧而不好学，其流弊是荡逸；好诚信而不好学，其流弊是最终害己；好直率而不好学，其流弊是语言尖刻伤人；好勇敢而不好学，其流弊是作乱；好刚强而不好学，其流弊是狂妄。"❷孔子自己"十五岁有志于学问"❸，最终成就了圣人人格。孔子通过自己的人生

❶ 见《论语·宪问》。
❷ 见《论语·阳货》。
❸ 见《论语·为政》。

❶ See "Xianwen," *Lunyu*.
❷ See "Yang Huo," *Lunyu*.
❸ See "Weizheng," *Lunyu*.

explained that his accomplishments were not due to a heavenly gift or an endowment of the spirits but something he had acquired himself through study. When Confucius studied, he had no regular teacher. He said, "When three persons walk together, one of them is worthy of my emulation." ❶ Confucius not only regarded study as the means of acquiring knowledge and of elevating character, he also regarded it as a spiritual search and a kind of enjoyment. He said, "To study and constantly review, isn't this a happy thing?" ❷ He hoped that he himself would "strive to study without becoming weary, and to teach others without tiring." ❸ This aspect explains that learning is decisively significant for molding the character and for human growth. In another aspect, through personal experience, Confucius thoroughly marked off the boundaries of religion and theology. Confucius was not born to be some sort of natural founding patriarch; rather, he achieved the character of a sage or worthy through study on his own. He lectured students on study methods and how to be a person, not like a religious patriarch who dispensed the will of god to his followers. Therefore, Confucius was an educationalist, not a patriarch. Confucius' experiences and his search for the development of human character profoundly influenced the fundamental nature and direction of Chinese culture.

Next is regarding the content of education. In the main, Confucius educated students in "written works, conduct, loyalty, and faithfulness." ❹ What is known as "written works" are the *Book of Poetry*, the *Book of Documents*, the *Rites*, the *Book of Music*, as well as what he taught late in life, the *Book of Changes*, and the *Spring and Autumn Annals*. These are known as the "Six Arts" (revered later as the "Six Classics"). These concern education for knowledge and for learning. As far as Confucius was concerned, each of the "Six Arts" had their own points of emphasis, and strengths and weaknesses, and each had their dissimilar uses. At the same time, Confucius did not completely believe in books, and especially pointed out which aspects one should emphasize while studying the "Six Arts." As for the *Book of Poetry*, one has to understand change and not be misled into "ignorance" ; as for the *Book of Documents*, one has to be open-minded and not be "deceived" ; as for the *Book of Music*, one has to know what is the proper degree and not be misled into "luxury" ; as for the *Book of Changes*, one cannot be trapped by the mysterious and the strange, and be misled into becoming "cunning" ; as for the *Rites*, one cannot lend it excessive veneration and be misled by the "details" ; and as for the *Spring and Autumn Annals*, one cannot wantonly praise and blame, and be

经历，说明了他的成就并非来自于天赋或神授，是通过后天的学习而成。孔子学无常师，他说："三个人在一起走，其中便一定有值得我学习的人。"❶孔子不但将学习作为获取知识、提升人格的手段，而且视为精神追求与享受，他说："学习并时常温习，不是很高兴的事吗？"❷希望自己"努力学习而不厌弃，教导别人而不疲倦"。❸这一方面说明了学习对于人格的塑造、人的成长具有决定性的意义；另一方面，孔子通过自身的经历，彻底划清了与宗教神学的界限。孔子并不是天生的通天教主，他是通过后天的学习而成就圣贤品格的。他向学生讲授的是学习和做人的方法，而不像宗教教主那样向信徒们宣说神的旨意，因此，孔子是教育家而非教主，孔子的经历和他对人格修养的追求，深刻地影响了中国文化的基本品格和走向。

再次，关于教学内容。孔子教育学生主要是"文、行、忠、信"❹几个方面。所谓"文"，就是《诗》、《书》、《礼》、《乐》，以及晚年所教的《易》、《春秋》，也就是"六艺"（后世尊为"六经"），这是知识与学问的教育。在孔子看来，"六艺"各有侧重，得失不同，各有不尽相同的作用。同时，孔子并不尽信书本，还特别提出了学习"六艺"应该注意的方面：对于《诗》不能不知变化而失之于"愚"，对于《书》不能不知存疑而失之于"诬"，对于《乐》不能不知有度而失之于"奢"，对于《易》不能陷于隐晦怪异而失之于"贼"，对于《礼》不能过度遵从而失之于"烦"，对于《春秋》不能妄为褒贬而失之

❶ 见《论语·述而》。
❷ 见《论语·学而》。
❸ 见《论语·述而》。
❹《论语·述而》。

❶ See "Shu'er," *Lunyu.*
❷ See "Xue'er," *Lunyu.*
❸ See "Shu'er," *Lunyu.*
❹ "Shu'er," *Lunyu.*

mislead into being "rebellious." It is evident that Confucius engaged in penetrating research and practical analysis of the "Six Arts" ; his purpose was to attempt to gain benefits and not be harmed while garnering the best educational results. Among the "Six Arts" one can gain knowledge through study as well as be influenced emotionally while engaging in moral cultivation. Confucius not only provided keen thinking on the "Six Arts," but also put forward a warning against learning with no thought to personal improvement. "Conduct," so called, was a kind of practical education as well as standardized behavior that enabled one to take one's place in society. For instance, Confucius emphasized "ritual," demanding that students avoid rebellious behavior. He said, "Do not look at behavior not in keeping with ritual; do not listen to words not in keeping with ritual; do not say things not in keeping with ritual; and do not do things not in keeping with ritual." ❶ As far as "conduct" goes, Confucius stressed the need to handle the relationships between "speech" and "conduct," and "learning" and "conduct" ; that is, the way to endow the ideal with the practical. "Loyalty" and "trustworthiness" are principles pertaining to human relations and politics. They are part of moral education.

Finally, let's discuss Confucius' method of education. Confucius advocated the integration of study and thought. He not only required students to study the knowledge at hand, but also strove to enlighten their abilities to think independently. The former was based on reverence for the essence of the culture; the latter was the premise of creating new knowledge. Just how to handle the relationship between "study" and "thought" is a question that must be effectively resolved at an educational activity. Concerning this, Confucius advocated the utilization and integration of both study and thought; he said, "Study without thought is losing effort; but thought without study is dangerous." ❷ This means that if one studies without any reflection, then such effort will be wasted; but if one only reflects without any effort to study, then it will be very dangerous. "Learning" indicates the reception and accumulation of knowledge; "thought" then is theoretical analysis and logical inference; both of these combine to form the activity of learning. Confucius stressed the integration of study and thought; this revealed the internal rules of study and the interactive relationship between knowledge and thought. This exerted an important influence on ancient Chinese education. This was especially so with regard to the tradition of education that stressed great breadth of knowledge; Confucius stressed the interaction of "study" and "thought" in this tradition, which bore great significance in developing creative thinking in students. The following is an exchange between Confucius and his disciple Zigong.

于"乱"。可见，孔子对"六艺"进行了深入的研究和实事求是的分析，目的是企求有得而无失，获得最佳的教学效果。"六艺"之中既有知识的学习，也有性情的熏染，道德的修养。孔子既有对"六艺"精妙思想的提示，也有防止学而不化的警戒。所谓"行"，就是立身处世的行为规范以及实践教育，如，孔子重视"礼"，要求学生不要做违礼的事，他说："不合礼的事不看，不合礼的话不听，不合礼的话不说，不合礼的事不做。"❶ 在"行"这方面，孔子强调的是要处理好"言"与"行"、"学"与"行"之间的关系，也就是将理想付之于实践的方法。"忠"、"信"则是人伦政治原则，是道德教育。

最后，关于教学方法。孔子主张学、思结合。既要求学生学习现成的知识，又努力启发学生自己思考。前者是基于对文化精粹的敬畏，后者则是知识创新的前提。如何处理好"学"与"思"的关系，这是教育活动中需要认真解决的问题。对此，孔子主张学思并举、学思结合，他说："学而不思则罔，思而不学则殆。"❷ 意思是说，只读书而不思考，就会陷于迷惘；只思考而不读书，同样是很危险的。"学"是指知识的接受与积累，"思"则是理论分析与逻辑推理，这两者共同组成了学习活动。孔子强调学思结合，揭示了学习的内在规律和知识与思想之间的互动关系，对中国古代教育产生了重要的影响。尤其是在注重博学多识的教育传统中，孔子揭示"思"与"学"的互动，对于培养学生的创造性思维具有重要意义。孔子与弟

❶ 见《论语·颜渊》。
❷《论语·为政》。

❶ See "Yan Yuan," *Lunyu*.
❷ "Weizheng," *Lunyu*.

Confucius asked Zigong, "Do you think that I am a person of great breadth of knowledge?" Zigong responded, "Yes. Isn't this so?" Confucius said, "No. I have one line of thought, one principle that runs through all of my learning." ❶ What Confucius meant by this "single thread" obviously meant the thinking and principles obtained through extrapolation and summary. That is to say, Confucius was not satisfied by his great breadth of learning; keen thinking was even more important. Of course, thought and study are like two wheels on the same cart; neither can be dispensed with. Thought without study is likewise of no benefit. The accumulation of knowledge is the premise as well as the foundation of mental extrapolation. He said, "I once spent an entire day and night on thought, neither eating nor sleeping, but it was all in vain; it is better to study." ❷ It is evident that Confucius equally advocated both study and thought, a learning method of study and thought combined into one unity. Confucius used the pedagogical methods of enlightening and attracting the interest of his students; but unless students expressed interest in seeking understanding for themselves but had gone as far as they could go, he would not instruct them on how to proceed; unless students had progressed to the point of wanting to articulate what they had learned yet were unable to do so, he would not enlighten them. At the same time, knowledge is limitless, so the key to educational activities was to develop in students the ability to acquire learning, to cause students to be able to learn how to perceive more than can be learned by limited study methods, to grasp a category and by extension what is related to this category. Confucius said, "If I lift one corner but they don' t reciprocate with the other three, then I don' t repeat myself." ❸ This means that if he indicated one direction of a problem, but a student could not extrapolate the other three directions, then Confucius would not continue teaching; the student would have to first resolve the problem of how to extrapolate. Confucius stressed developing the self-initiative and the pro-activeness of students, and emphasized the study method of extrapolation. This was of great significance.

Confucius' teaching emphasized the methodology of integrating study with thought; the purpose was for the sake of cultivating the self-initiative of students. He encouraged students to be brave in upholding the truth, not to blindly believe their teachers; therefore, the process of teaching was a process that benefited both teacher and learner. From the *Analects* we can see that, in the main, Confucius adopted the format of question and answer in his teaching where the teacher and student held discussions. The premise of education that benefited both teacher and student fostered an environment of relative equality

子子贡有这样一段对话，孔子问子贡说："你以为我是博学多识的人吗？"子贡说："是的，难道不是这样吗？"孔子说："不是，我有统摄知识的一以贯之的思想与原则。"❶孔子所说的"一以贯之"，显然是指经过推理与概括而得出的思想与原则，也就是说，孔子自己并不以博学多识而自满，精思才是更重要的。当然，思与学如同车之两轮，不可偏废，思而不学，同样无益。知识的积累是思考推理的前提与基础，他说："我曾经整天不吃饭、整夜不睡地去思考，但徒劳无益，不如去学习。"❷可见，孔子提倡的是学思并重、学思一体的学习方法。孔子还以启发诱导的方式进行教学，不到学生想求明白而不能的时候，不去提示他；不到学生想说却说不出的时候，不去启发他。同时，知识是无限的，教学活动关键是培养学生获取知识的能力，使学生能够通过有限的知识学习，掌握举一反三、触类旁通的本领。孔子说："举一隅，不以三隅反，则不复也。"❸就是说，如果给学生指明一个方向，他不能推理出其它三个方向，就不能再教下去了，而应该首先解决推理方法的问题。孔子注意培养学生的主动性、积极性，重视推理方法的教学手段，很具现实意义。

孔子教学注意学思结合的方法，目的是要培养学生的自主意识。他鼓励学生勇于坚持真理，不迷信老师，因此，教学的过程也是教学相长的过程。从《论语》中我们可以看出，孔子的教学主要采取问答的形式，师生商论。教学相长的前提是师

❶ 见《论语·卫灵公》。
❷ 见《论语·卫灵公》。
❸《论语·述而》。

❶ See "Weilinggong," *Lunyu*.
❷ See "Weilinggong," *Lunyu*.
❸ "Shu'er," *Lunyu*.

between teacher and student. From the records in the *Analects* we can observe that Confucius and his students were rather equal; students could relax and initiate conversations with Confucius at will. Many times Zilu offered advice to Confucius concerning his conduct, and Confucius accepted each of them. For instance, the family steward of the Ji clan, Gongshan Furao wanted to summon Confucius; as Confucius was preparing to go to see Gongshan Furao, he ultimately was dissuaded from going by Zilu. One time his disciples embarrassed him, but Confucius did not become enraged. For instance, the wife of Duke Ling of Wei, Nanzi, had a bad reputation; she desired to see Confucius so Confucius felt compelled to go to meet with her. Zilu was unhappy about this, so Confucius had to swear an oath before Heaven of his innocence. All of this embodies the equal and harmonious relationship between Confucius and his students. This allowed students to feel that they could say anything they liked, and offer their own views. Confucius pointed out, "In matters of humaneness, do not yield to your teacher." ❶ This is the notion that in aspects concerning humanness, decide yourself even if it means going against your teacher; this embodies the spirit of equality. The *Analects* records a large number of situations with students asking questions and Confucius answering them. At the same time, many scenarios exist consisting of free exchanges of discussion. Many of Confucius' teaching activities involving interactions between teachers and students, and the mutual posing of questions, appear quite frequently, such as the following one. When Confucius and Ran You were crossing through the state of Wei, they saw that the population was very dense. Ran You asked, "With such a large population, what should one do?" Confucius answered, "Enrich them." Ran You asked further, "After they become enriched, then what?" Confucius said, "Educate them." ❷ In responding to Ran You's queries, Confucius' answers were replete in political wisdom and philosophical thought. Opposite to this was when Confucius brought up the question, and students provided the answers that led to even more profound ones. For instance, when Confucius was together with Yan Yuan and Zilu, Confucius posed the question, "Why don' t each of you express your own aspirations?" Zilu spoke first, "To share my chariot, horses, and clothing with my friends, and even if they get damaged, to have no regrets." Yan Yuan said, "I desire to avoid praising my own strong points, and not draw attention to my own merits." Afterwards, Zilu asked Confucius what were his own aspirations. Confucius said, "My aspirations are to give ease to the aged, to treat friends with trustworthiness, and cause the young to long for me." ❸ This particular exchange of questions and answers is a process of

生具有较为平等的环境，从《论语》的记载可以看出，孔子与学生是颇为平等的，弟子可以轻松随和地与孔子进行讨论。子路多次对孔子的行为提出忠告，孔子都一一接受了，如季氏家臣公山弗扰想召孔子去，孔子准备前往，但最终还是被子路劝阻了。有时，弟子还使孔子颇为尴尬，但孔子并不愤怒，如卫灵公夫人南子名声不好，她想见孔子，孔子勉强去相见，对此，子路不高兴，孔子不得已而对天发誓。这一切都体现了孔子与弟子之间平等、融洽的关系，从而使得学生能够畅所欲言，提出自己的见解。孔子提出："当仁，不让于师。"❶在仁德面前，即使是对老师也不谦让，体现了平等的精神。《论语》中有大量学生发问、孔子作答的内容，同时还有很多平等讨论的情景。孔子的教学活动师生互动、互相发问的情形屡见不鲜，如孔子与冉有在经过卫国的路上，看到卫国的人口十分稠密，冉有问："人口多了，还应该怎么办？"孔子回答说："使他们富裕。"冉有又问："已经富裕了，又该怎么办？"孔子说："教育他们。"❷针对冉有的提问，孔子的回答富含深刻的政治智慧和哲学思考。反之，也有孔子发问、学生作答而后引向深入的，如孔子与颜渊、子路在一起，孔子提出："何不说说各人的志向呢？"子路先说道："将我的车马衣服与朋友共享，即使坏了也无憾。"颜渊说："我愿不夸耀自己的好处，不表白自己的功劳。"其后，子路又问孔子的志向，孔子说："我的志向是使老者安逸，使朋友信任，使年轻人怀念我。"❸这一问答过程是志向不断递

❶《论语·卫灵公》。
❷ 见《论语·子路》。
❸ 见《论语·公冶长》。

❶ "Weilinggong," *Lunyu*.
❷ See "Zilu," *Lunyu*.
❸ See "Gongye Chang," *Lunyu*.

elevating aspirations. Confucius' aspirations were elevated on the foundations laid by Zilu and Yan Yuan. It is hard to say whether Confucius enlightened his students or his students enlightened him; nor is it really necessary to say. This is the highest point reached in Confucius' approach to teaching of benefiting both teacher and student. Learning is a happy process of teacher/student discussion. Therefore, when a teacher "teaches others without weariness," students then "learn without weariness." Confucius highly stressed nurturing the interest of students in learning. He said, "(Concerning learning) understanding it is not as good as delighting in it, and delighting in it is not as good as regarding it as a source of happiness." ❶ The best learning situation is to make it joyful. Confucius said further, "To learn and constantly review it, isn't this joyful?" ❷

Confucius' students were numerous, yet their personalities and abilities were different, so were their study methods and the goals they were working towards. Confucius was able to enact a curriculum and methodology according to these different characteristics, to achieve the best educational results. Zhu Xi of the Song Dynasty said, "The master (referring to Confucius) taught each student according to his talent." ❸ This is what later generations referred to as to teach according to talent. The premise of teaching according to talent is a complete understanding of each student. In the *Analects* Confucius is often seen as discussing the differences between his disciples. Some examples are, Confucius felt that Zilu could be entrusted with the troops and the military affairs of a state of a thousand military chariots, and Ran Qiu could be the magistrate of a county with a population of one thousand households or could be the commander of a hundred military chariots. Wearing ritual costume and standing in the middle of the court, Gongxi Chi could be sent to receive guests and handle diplomatic affairs. "Xianjin" in the *Analects* mentions that Confucius' curriculum included the four categories of moral conduct, language, political affairs, and literature. Yan Yuan and three others were known for their superior moral conduct, Zai Wo and Zigong were good at verbal skills, Ran You and Jilu were best at political affairs, and Ziyou and Zixia had mastered "literature" (including culture, written records, regulations, and institutions and the like). These characterizations were made based completely on the individual strengths of the students, not because of the curricular categories established by Confucius. Confucius' evaluations and comparisons of the talents and temperament of his students are frequently seen in the *Analects*. For example, Zigong once asked Confucius, who was better,

升的过程，孔子的志向正是在子路与颜渊的基础上的升华。是孔子启发了学生，还是学生启发了孔子，已难以辨析，也不用辨析了，这是孔子师生教学相长达到的最佳境界。学习是师生之间切磋商论的愉快过程，因此，老师"诲人不倦"，学生则"学而不厌"。孔子十分注重培养学生的学习兴趣，他说："（对于学习）懂得的不如喜爱的，喜爱的不如以其为乐的。"❶最佳的学习状况是以学习为快乐。孔子还说："学而时习之，不亦说乎？"❷意思是说：学习并时常温习，不是很快乐吗？

孔子的学生众多，学生的个性、能力各有不同，学习的方法与培养的目标也不同，孔子能够根据学生不同的特征，实施因人而异的教学内容与方法，取得最优的教学效果。宋代的朱熹说："夫子（指孔子）教人，各因其材"❸，也就是后世所说的因材施教。因材施教的前提是对学生要有充分的了解。在《论语》中时常见到孔子谈到弟子的差异。如，孔子认为子路可负责有一千辆兵车的国家的兵役和军政工作，而冉求则可以做千户人口的县长、百辆兵车的大夫总管，公西赤穿着礼服，立于朝廷之中，可以让他接待外宾，办理交涉。《论语·先进篇》里提到孔子教学有德行、言语、政事、文学四科。颜渊等四人德行优秀，宰我、子贡善于辞令，冉有、季路擅长政事，子游与子夏精通"文学"（文化、典籍、典章、制度等）。这完全是因学生个人的特长而提出的，并不是孔子事先设定的科目。《论语》中时常见到孔子对于学生才情的品评与比较。如，子贡问孔子：子张与子夏两人哪一个

❶ 见《论语·雍也》。
❷《论语·学而》。
❸《四书章句集注·论语集注》。

❶ See "Yongye," *Lunyu.*
❷ "Xue'er," *Lunyu.*
❸ "Lunyu Jizhu," in *Sishu Zhangju Jizhu.*

Zizhang or Zixia? Confucius responded to him, saying that Zizhang was somewhat excessive, while Zixia was somewhat backwards. One should adopt different educational methodologies and educational contents for students of different abilities and personalities. Confucius said that an above average student can be taught lofty and profound learning, but a below average student cannot be taught this lofty and profound learning. Teaching according to the abilities of students was often embodied in how Confucius carried out his educational program, for Confucius constantly gave dissimilar responses to the same questions, based on the different characteristics of students. For instance, Yan Yuan, Zhonggong, Sima Niu, and Fan Chi all asked Confucius about the content of the way of "humaneness" ; Confucius' answers to each of them were different. Even more evident was when Zilu and Ran You both asked Confucius, saying, is it true that if one hears about something that should be done, it should be done immediately? When Confucius answered Zilu, he said, if your father and elder brother are still alive, how can you act immediately? Yet when he responded to Ran You, he said, when hearing about something that should be done, then one should do it immediately. Gongxi Hua did not understand this, and asked Confucius why he gave two different responses. Confucius said, usually Ran You is reticent, so I encouraged him and urged him on; but Zilu likes to surpass others, and is bold in taking action, so I want to slow down his actions. This is a typical case of personalized instruction.

Through establishing private schools, the educational thought that Confucius distilled with its rich content, together with the education for commoners that he inaugurated, all pointed the way to the fundamental direction of the development of education in ancient China. Some of the vital contents of Confucius' educational thought up to the present are still worthy of our learning and instruction.

更好一些？孔子回答他，子张有些过分，子夏有些赶不上。对于不同才能、不同性情的学生，应该采取不同的教育方法、教学内容。孔子说过，中等水平以上的人，可以告诉他高深的学问，中等水平以下的人，不可以告诉他高深学问。因材施教在孔子的教学实践中时有体现，孔子经常对同样的问题，根据学生的不同特点予以不尽相同的回答。如，颜渊、仲弓、司马牛、樊迟都曾向孔子问"仁"道的内容，孔子的回答各有不同。更明显的是，子路与冉有都问孔子：是否听到该做的事就立即做起来？孔子回答子路时说，有父亲和哥哥活着，怎可以立即就做起来呢？而回答冉有时则说，听到该做的事就应该立即做起来。对此，公西华十分不解，问孔子为什么有两种不同的答案。孔子说，冉有平时做事退缩，所以我给他鼓励，劝进；子路喜欢胜人，勇于作为，所以我要延缓他的行为。这是典型的个性化教学的案例。

孔子通过兴办私学总结出来的丰富的教育思想，以及他首创的平民教育，指明了中国古代教育发展的基本路向。孔子教育思想中某些富有生命力的内容，直到今天仍值得我们学习和借鉴。

孔子和弟子们

Confucius and his disciples

九 "修己以安百姓"——孔子的德治思想

Chapter IX " Cultivate the Self in Order to Ease
 the People" : Confucius' Thought
 on Moral Rule

Although Confucius was not entrusted with important responsibilities by contemporary rulers, his thought possessed a strong spirit of realism. This was embodied in particular in his political thought. Confucius based this on ethics, for his political thought had a rather distinct ethical hue. As far as Confucius was concerned, the premise of politics was self-cultivation to become a sage. When Ji Kangzi asked Confucius about politics, he answered, saying, "To govern means to correct. If you lead by being correct, who would dare to not be correct?" ❶ This means that so-called politics, requires first of all that rulers be morally upright; first accomplishing one's ideal character, then one will be able to realize an ideal government. If the one in power himself is upright, who would dare not to be upright? Confucius also said, if the ruler is personally upright, then the government could be run even without any orders or commands. But if one were not personally upright, even with orders and commands, no one would obey them. In the *Analects*, Confucius often stated that the foundation of government lay in the cultivation of morality on the part of the ruler. He said, "Using virtue to enact governance, the ruler himself is like the north star, in its own set position with other stars revolving around it." ❷ Confucius pointed out that "enacting governance by means of virtue" is none other than "rule through virtue." This means that the one in power must be good in moral cultivation. Concerning this, Confucius put forward a series of principles for moral rule.

First is about the ideal realms of the moral rules of Yao, Shun, King Wen of Zhou and King Wu of Zhou. What Confucius meant by moral rule was the result of self-cultivation on the part of rulers, it did not refer to a pre-set political purpose. Therefore, the inward cultivation of moral conduct was fundamental; the achievement of an ideal government was the outer manifestation of this type of cultivation. Ethical thought was the foundation; thought on education and politics were both the embodiments of different realms in this ethical thought. Confucius lived in a period of great upheaval. At the time states were being swallowed up, and regicide and fratricide were very common; this condition was the complete antithesis to Confucius' ideal government. Therefore, he took the ancient sage kings Yao and Shun as his models, and through glamorizing the view of ancient society, he invested his political ideals in them. He described the legendary times of Yao and Shun as the "utopian" age, with "equal justice for all." He regarded this as the acme of his ideals. The age of the "Six Lords," Yu, Tang, Wen, Wu, King Cheng and the Duke of Zhou, was the age when the "Great Way operated with stability," with "equal justice for all," in an era of "prosperity." The period of West Zhou,

　　孔子虽然不被当政者重用,但其思想具有强烈的现实精神,这在其政治思想中体现得尤为突出。孔子以伦理为本,其政治思想也具有鲜明的伦理色彩。在孔子看来,政治是以修己成圣为前提的,当季康子向孔子问政治时,孔子回答说:"政者,正也。子帅以正,孰敢不正。"❶意思是说,所谓政治,首先是执政者要品行端正,先成就自己的理想人格,然后才能实现理想政治。如果执政者身正,谁敢不端正呢?孔子还说统治者如果身正,没有教令,也可推行;如果自身不正,虽有教令,也没有人信从。在《论语》中孔子时常说政治的根本在于统治者修养自己的品德,他说:"以道德来施行政治,自己就好像北极星一样,在一定的位置上,其他的星辰都环绕它。"❷孔子提出"为政以德",也就是"德治",是指执政者需具有良好的道德修养。对此,孔子提出了一系列的道德政治原则。

　　首先,以尧、舜、周文王、周武王为德治的理想境界。孔子所说的德治是为政者自我修养的结果,并不是预设的政治目的。因此,内修德行是根本,理想政治的实现是这种修养的外化。孔子以伦理思想为本,教育、政治等思想都是伦理思想在不同领域的体现。孔子所处的是一个大动荡的时期,当时列国兼并、弑君杀父、兄弟相残的现象十分普遍,与孔子的理想政治相差太远,因此,他便以远古的帝王尧、舜作为标准,通过美化古代的社会图景来寄托政治理想。他将传说中的尧舜时代描述成"天下为公"的"大同"时代,并以此作为理想的最高境界,而禹、汤、文、武、成王、周公这"六君子"的时代则是"大道既隐,天下为家"的"小康"时代。他极其仰慕的典

❶《论语·颜渊》。
❷ 见《论语·为政》。

❶ "Yan Yuan," *Lunyu*.
❷ See "Weizheng," *Lunyu*.

which Confucius was greatly admired and whose culture of regulations, institutions, rituals, and music was well reserved, belonged to the era of "prosperity." The "utopian" world of Yao and Shun described by Confucius was realized through the natural utilization of the internal morality of rulers. Therefore, it was colored with some elements akin to natural, non-purposeful action. He said, "How great was Yao! Only Heaven is the greatest and biggest. Only Yao could model himself on Heaven. Oh, his grace is so vast that the people are unable to praise him adequately. The virtue of his merits are truly lofty, and his cultural brilliance is completely beautiful." ❶ When describing Shun, Confucius said, "Probably only Shun was able to govern through non-purposeful action, right? What did he do? He only sat solemnly and upright in his court." ❷ In Confucius' view, the realization of the utopian society of Yao and Shun was not in the main achieved by any effort in political affairs but rather in the internal strength of their characters and the glory of their virtues. Their moral rules were due merely to the externalization of their lofty virtues. Confucius' models for a "prosperous society" whom he venerated so much— the kings of the Zhou Dynasty— were also enlightened lords of virtuous conduct and high probity. He once sighed, "The virtue of the Zhou Dynasty can be termed the loftiest." ❸ The "rites" that he desired to restore were the rites of Zhou. What he stated about "Overcoming the self and returning to the rites is humaneness" obviously expressed the relationship between "overcoming the self," cultivating "humaneness" and restoring the rites of the Zhou. Confucius' high level of approbation of the civilization of the West Zhou was due chiefly to that fact that Zhou had enlightened monarchs such as King Wen and King Wu with their high degrees of cultivation. When Duke Ai of Lu, the lord of the state of Lu, discussed politics with Confucius, Confucius stated the following, "The governments of Wen and Wu, were found in the local histories; when they were alive, then the government was elevated; when they were dead, then good government disappeared." ❹ This means that the political accomplishments of Kings Wen and Wu were recorded in historical records; when they were alive, then political accomplishments were very evident, but when they were dead, then political accomplishments ceased. A "utopian world" was the ideal goal that Confucius sought; but a "prosperous world" was the practical goal that he sought. The realization of an ideal government was based on the premise of the moral quality of its political rulers, especially its lord kings.

章制度、礼乐文明保存较好的西周时代就属于"小康"时代。孔子所描述的尧、舜的"大同"之世是通过统治者内在德性的自然发挥与运用而实现的，因此，也带有某种自然无为的色彩。他说："伟大啊，尧。只有天最高最大，只有尧能够以天为法式。他的恩泽真是浩荡啊，乃至民众无法赞美。他的功德实在太崇高了，他的文化光彩也十分美好。"❶ 在描写舜时，孔子说："能够无为而治的，大概只有舜吧？他做些什么呢？只是庄严端正地坐在朝廷上而已。"❷ 在孔子看来，尧、舜大同社会的实现，主要不在于勤政有为，而主要在于尧、舜内在的人格力量、道德光辉，他们的德治只不过是他们高尚德性的外化而已。孔子所崇尚的"小康"之世的典范——周朝的君王，也是德行高尚的明君，他感叹道："周朝的道德，可说是最高的了。"❸ 他所要复兴的"礼"，就是周礼，他所谓"克己复礼为仁"，明确地表现了"克己"与修"仁"德和复兴周礼的关系。孔子高度推崇的西周文明，关键是有周文王、周武王那样修养极好的明君。鲁国君主鲁哀公与孔子谈论政治时，孔子说过这样的话："文武之政，布在方策，其人存，则其政举；其人亡，则其政息。"❹ 意思是说，周代文王、武王的政绩记载在文献上。他们人在，政绩就显现；他们人不在，政绩就结束。"大同"之世是孔子追求的理想目标，"小康"之世则是孔子追求的现实目标。理想政治的实现是以为政者尤其是君王的道德素质为基本前提的。

❶ 见《论语·泰伯》。
❷ 见《论语·卫灵公》。
❸ 见《论语·泰伯》。
❹ 见《礼记·中庸》。

❶ See "Taibo," *Lunyu*.
❷ See "Weilinggong," *Lunyu*.
❸ See "Taibo," *Lunyu*.
❹ See "Zhongyong," *Liji*.

Next is concerning self-cultivation (cultivation of personal moral conduct) and elevating the worthy. In the *Analects*, one exchange of questions and answers between Zilu and Confucius explains that a gentleman who participates in government should base himself on self-cultivation.

> Zilu asked how one could become a gentleman. Confucius said, "Cultivate your own virtue; solemnly and assiduously attend to your work." Zilu further asked, "Is this all?" Confucius said, "Cultivate your own virtue to cause those above you to be at ease and happy." Zilu asked yet again, "Is this all?" Confucius said, "Cultivate your own virtue to cause all the people to be at ease and happy. Of course, it is not easy to cultivate your own virtue to cause all the people to be at ease and happy. Yao and Shun probably were not able to do it completely." ❶

To Confucius, "easing the people" is a difficult task sought by the gentleman, and it is possible that this highest achievement will not be reached. The fundamental premise behind "easing the people" is "self-cultivation." Moral cultivation on the part of those in government is the precondition for achieving an orderly and lawful government. Cultivation of character on the part of those in government often plays an important and a leading role in improving social mores and the political environment. When Ji Kangzi, the political power in the state of Lu, asked Confucius about politics, he asked how should one handle the large amount of robbers? Confucius said, "If you are not greedy for wealth and goods, people would not steal even if you encouraged them to do so." Ji Kangzi again asked Confucius, "What if I killed the bad and kept close to the good, how would that be?" Confucius said, "Since you govern the state, why should you kill people? If you want to govern the state in a good manner, then the people will naturally become good. The virtuous conduct of those in power is like the wind, and the virtuous conduct of the people is like the grass; wherever the wind blows, the grass will bend in that direction." ❷The principles of enacting government proposed by Confucius were all based on the moral cultivation of those in power. What is worth noticing is that Confucius distinguished between "easing the people" and "easing the commoners." What he called the "people" were those in the upper levels above the knights and grandees as opposed to the "commoners." Confucius' setting the "commoners" above the level of the "people" embodied a fresh type of people-based thinking. At the same time, for the ultimate pursuit of the "gentleman," Confucius advocated "easing the people" over "governing the state and the world" ; this embodied Confucius' thought on

其次，修己（修养自己的德行）与举贤。《论语》中子路与孔子有一段问答，说明君子为政应当以修己为本。

> 子路问怎样才能做一个君子。孔子说："修养自己的品德，严肃认真地对待工作。"子路又问："这样就可以了吗？"孔子说："修养自己的品德使上层人物得以安乐。"子路又问："这样就可以了吗？"孔子说："修养自己使所有的百姓得以安乐。当然，修养自己使百姓得以安乐很不容易，尧舜大概也没有能够完全做到。"❶

在孔子看来，"安百姓"是君子苦苦追求，但可能无法达到的最高境界。"安百姓"的基本前提是"修己"，为政者个人的道德修养是实现政治清明的条件。为政者自身的人格修养往往对社会风气、政治环境产生重要的表率作用。当鲁国的执政者季康子问政于孔子时，季康子问盗贼多怎么办？孔子说："如果您不贪求财货，即使奖励也没有人偷盗。"季康子又问孔子："杀掉坏人而亲近好人，怎么样？"孔子说："您治理国家，为什么要杀人？您想治理好国家，百姓就会好起来。执政者的德行好像是风，百姓的德行好像草。风向哪里吹，草便向哪里倒。"❷ 孔子提出的为政原则，都是以为政者本身的道德修养为基础的。值得注意的是，孔子将"安人"与"安百姓"区分开来，所谓"人"是指与"民"、"百姓"相对的士大夫以上的上层阶层。孔子将"百姓"置于"人"之上，体现了鲜明的民本思想。同时，孔子以"安百姓"而不是"治国平天下"为"君子"的至上追求，体现了孔子

❶ 见《论语·宪问》。

❷ 见《论语·颜渊》。

❶ See "Xianwen," *Lunyu.*

❷ See "Yan Yuan," *Lunyu.*

regarding the people as the foundation. Even though "governing the state and the world" perhaps included some elements of moral rule, nevertheless doubtlessly the rule of law was a more important aspect. What Confucius said about "easing the commoners" took as its goal the survival and rights of the people, including their emotions and aspirations. "To ease" implies both physical as well as emotional comfort; it means both to insure the survival and rights of the common people as well as to safeguard their human dignity. The reason one can bring about such effects lies in the fact that both "self-cultivation" as well as "easing the people" are based on the virtue of "humaneness" ; both are permeated with a moral content. "Self-cultivation" and "easing the people" enjoy the relationship shared between a method and a goal. "Self-cultivation and easing the people" is not only the ideal of Confucius' educational program, but also a political ideal. As far as its basic nature goes, it pertains to the realm of an educational ideal. This then is the one "thread" of Confucius' way of "humaneness."

While the worthy cultivate their virture, it is also necessary for those in power to elevate the worthy and to employ the able, and make the worthy feel that they are honored. The significance of all of this is that the view towards personnel is an important structural component of political thought. When Confucius discussed the political importance of the right personnel, he said, "With the right personnel, the government will flourish; without the right personnel, good government will cease." Therefore, he felt that the foundation of government lay in good personnel. When Confucius' student Zhonggong was serving as the family steward to the Ji clan, he asked Confucius' advice about how to engage in government. Confucius answered that three aspects were necessary: First, be a good example; second, do not pay attention to the petty faults of others; third, elevate and employ superior personnel. When Duke Ai of Lu asked Confucius how to make the people submit to him, Confucius said, "Elevate and employ the upright, and dismiss those not upright, then the people will submit; if you elevate and employ those who are not upright, and dismiss the upright, then the masses will not submit." ❶ Confucius felt that promoting and elevating the worthy should also become a common practice throughout society. When Zhonggong asked Confucius how one would be able to distinguish superior talent and then promote them, Confucius said, "Promote those whom you know; as for those you do not know, how could it be that others will keep them hidden?" ❷ As for the standard of personnel, Confucius advocated the possession of both morality and talent, giving priority to morality. Confucius felt that "being thoroughly endowed with loyalty and

以百姓为本的德政思想。"治国平天下"虽然可能含有德治的内容，但法治无疑也是重要的方面，而孔子所说的"安百姓"是以百姓的生存权利，乃至百姓的情感意志为最终目标的。"安"，既有身安，也有心安的意味；既要保障百姓的生存权利，又要保障百姓的人格尊严。之所以能达到这一效果，在于"修己"与"安百姓"都是本于"仁"德，两者都贯注着道德的内涵。"修己"与"安百姓"是手段与目的的关系，"修己以安百姓"既是孔子的教育理想，也是政治理想，本质上，又是其伦理思想，这就是孔子"一贯"的"仁"道。

贤者内修品德，还需要执政者举贤用能，让贤者得到重用。从这个意义上说，人才观念也是政治思想的重要组成部分。孔子在谈及人才对于政治的重要时说："有人才存在，政治就兴旺；没有人才，则良好的政治就会停止。"因此，他认为政治的根本在于人才。孔子的学生仲弓做季氏的家臣，请教孔子如何为政，孔子回答他需做到三个方面：一是做好表率；二是不计较别人的小错误；三是举用优秀的人才。当鲁哀公问孔子如何才能使百姓心服时，孔子说："举用正直的人，罢免不正直的人，民众就心服；举用不正直的人，罢免正直的人，民众就不心服。"❶ 孔子认为，推举贤能还应形成普遍的社会风气。当仲弓问孔子怎样才能识别优秀人才，并将他们提拔出来时，孔子说："提拔你知道的，你不知道的，别人难道会埋没他吗？"❷ 对于人才的标准，孔子主张德才兼备，以德为先。孔子认为"忠信厚重"也就是具有"仁"德是人才的前

❶ 见《论语·为政》。
❷ 见《论语·子路》。

❶ See "Weizheng," *Lunyu.*
❷ See "Zilu," *Lunyu.*

honesty" was also the prerequisite to being an official of "humane" virtue. Those lacking these qualities are the same with jackals and wolves, and should not be approached. This embodied Confucius' rather comprehensive views on personnel. As far as the need to "judge their conduct," that is to judge whether or not their words match their deeds, which means that even the treacherous and fraudulent can be discovered. At the same time, one should not demand perfection of personnel; instead one should "overlook minor faults." This means one should not find fault over small errors, and should look at the big picture instead. Take Guan Zhong for instance. Although he had the minor faults of "not being frugal," and "did not know ritual," still his merit in government work was outstanding. Therefore, Confucius felt that Guan Zhong should still be considered as one of the "humane." As for the relationship between self-cultivation and employing others, as well as the role of elevating superior talent, the dialogue between Confucius and his disciple Fan Chi contained the following vivid and imaginative description:

> Fan Chi asked about humaneness, and Confucius said, "Love others." He then asked about knowledge; Confucius said, "Be good at judging others." But Fan Chi was still unable to completely understand, so Confucius said, "If you elevate the upright above the evil, then this will help the evil to turn upright." Fan Chi withdrew and went to see Zixia, saying, "I just went to see the master and asked him about wisdom; the master said, 'If you elevate the upright above the evil, then this will help the evil to turn upright.' What does this mean?" Zixia said, "How rich in meaning is this answer! After Shun gained all the world, he chose from among the people, and promoted Gao Yao, and the evil found it hard to survive. After Tang gained the world, he chose from among the people, and promoted Yi Yin, and the evil found it hard to survive." ❶

This clearly describes the self-cultivation of the virtue of "humaneness" on the part of the worthy as well as the course of using "wisdom" on the part of the rulers to elevate the worthy personnel; both concretely demonstrate the important role of elevating worthy personnel. It is evident that self-cultivation and the elevation of the worthy are the two most important factors in enacting moral government. Confucius' view on personnel is the extension of his moral view based on "humaneness" into the political realm; it is the externalization and expansion of "self-cultivation."

Next is about rule of virtue and comforting the people. Confucius undertook a comparison of the rule of virtue with the rule of law. He said, "If

提条件，不"忠信厚重"者就如同豺狼一般，不可靠近，这体现了孔子比较全面的人才观。对于人才还要"揆其行"，也就是测试其是否言行一致，这样，即使奸伪的人也能被发现。同时，对人才也不应求全责备，而应"赦小过"，就是不要计较小的错误，从大处着眼。如管仲，虽然有"不俭"、"不知礼"的"小过"，但政绩卓著，因此，孔子认为管仲仍然是"仁"者。关于修己与用人之间的关系以及举贤才的作用，孔子与弟子樊迟的一段对话中有生动形象的描述：

> 樊迟问仁，孔子说："爱人"；又问智，孔子说："善于鉴别人。"樊迟还不能透彻地理解，孔子说："把正直的人提拔到邪恶的人之上，就能够使邪恶的人正直。"樊迟退出来见到子夏，说："刚才我去向老师问智，老师说：'把正直的人提拔上来，位置在邪恶的人之上。'这是什么意思？"子夏说："这是内涵多么丰富的话啊！舜有了天下，在众人中挑选，将皋陶提拔出来，坏人就难以存在了；汤有了天下，在众人中挑选，把伊尹提拔上来，坏人也就难以存在了。"❶

这里清楚地描述了贤士自修"仁"德，执政者用"智"以举贤才的过程，并具体说明了举贤才的重要作用。可见，修己与举贤，是施行德治中最为重要的两个因素。孔子的人才观是他的以"仁"为本的道德观念在政治领域的延伸，是"修己"的外现及扩展。

❶ 见《论语·颜渊》。

❶ See "Yan Yuan," *Lunyu*.

you use the rule of law to lead the mass of the people and use punishments to restrain them, although the people will be able to avoid encroaching against the law, they will not have hearts of integrity. But if you use virtue to lead the mass of the people, and use ritual teachings to retrain them, then the people will not only have hearts of integrity, but also submit in their minds." ❶ Only through transforming the people by virtue will one be able to cause the people to understand integrity and humility and recognize the difference between honor and shame, and create from the bottom a harmonious, law-abiding social environment. Emphasizing virtue and slighting the law was the important characteristic of the political thought of Confucius and Confucian politicians. The most realistic manifestation of rigorously enacting the rule of virtue was the concern on the part of those in government for the troubles of the mass of the people, and to enact concrete policies to comfort the people. Confucius said, "To benefit the people where you are able, isn't this beneficial rather than wasteful? Choosing the best time to use the people in hard labor, who could complain about this?" ❷ He also said, "Governing a state of a thousand military chariots requires serious and assiduous attention to work, sincerity and trustworthiness with no deception, being frugal with expenditures, cherishing and protecting officials, and recruiting the people for public works when they have leisure time from their agricultural labor." ❸ Confucius felt that the moral transformation of the common people should proceed under the premise of a certain material foundation. On his way to the state of Wei while departing the state of Lu, he again discussed with Ran You that after the population increased one should enrich them; afterward one should transform them through education. He advocated teaching them after enriching them, feeling that material benefits should be the foundation for moral transformation. Although Confucius did not propose any concrete measures to enrich or benefit the people, he did advocate keeping the wealth among the people and reducing tax levies; that allowing the people to obtain practical benefits was the basis of the wealth of the state. When Duke Ai of Lu asked Confucius how to govern, Confucius said, "Store wealth among the people, reduce levies and the people will be enriched." ❹ Duke Ai of Lu asked Confucius' student You Ruo, "When the harvest is poor, and the resources of the state are insufficient, what should I do?" You Ruo said, "Why don't you enact the system of the tithe for your taxation?" Duke Ai answered, "Now a tax of twenty percent is not sufficient for our purposes, how can a tithe do?" You Ruo said, "If the people are enriched and sufficient, why isn't the lord of the state sufficient? If the people

再次，德治惠民。孔子将德治与法治进行对比，他说："以政法来引导民众，以刑罚来约束民众，民众虽然可以避免触犯法律，但并没有廉耻之心；如果用道德来引导民众，用礼教来约束民众，则民众不但具有廉耻之心，而且人心归服。"❶ 只有以德化民，才能使民众知廉耻，识荣辱，从根本上营造和谐守法的社会环境。重德而轻法，是孔子以及儒家政治思想的重要特征。励行德治，最现实的表现是为政者关心民众疾苦，实施具体的惠民政策。孔子说："就百姓可以获利之处使百姓获利，这不是获利而不浪费吗？选择百姓可以劳动的时间让他们去劳动，又有谁怨恨呢？"❷ 他又说："治理具有千辆兵车的国家，就要严肃认真地对待工作，诚信无欺，节约费用，爱护官吏，役使百姓要在农闲时间。"❸ 孔子认为，对百姓的道德教化应该在一定物质基础的前提下进行，在去卫国的路上，他与冉有谈到人口多了要使民众富起来，富了以后再实施教化。他主张富而后教，认为物质利益是德治教化的基础。孔子虽然没有提出具体的利民、富民措施，但他主张藏富于民，减少赋税，让民众得到实惠是国家富足之本。当鲁哀公问孔子如何为政时，孔子说："薄赋敛则民富。"❹ 鲁哀公问孔子的学生有若："年成不好，国家财物不足该怎么办？"有若说："为什么不实行十抽一的税率呢？"哀公回答说："现在十抽二还不够用，十抽一怎么够用呢？"有若则说："如果百姓

❶ 见《论语·为政》。
❷ 见《论语·尧曰》。
❸ 见《论语·学而》。
❹ 见《说苑》卷七《政理》。

❶ See "Weizheng," *Lunyu.*
❷ See "Yaoyue," *Lunyu.*
❸ See "Xue'er," *Lunyu.*
❹ "Zhengli," *Shuoyuan* Chaper Seven.

are poor, how can the lord of the state be enriched and sufficient?" ❶ What You Ruo said precisely embodies Confucius' thought on the rule of virtue and comforting the people. How can one enrich the people? Although Confucius rarely mentioned profit and he opposed "acting for the sake of personal interest," ❷ he did not avoid discussing "wealth," feeling that seeking a sufficiency of wealth is a common human instinct. He said, "Wealth and honor are what men naturally seek." ❸ As far as Confucius was concerned, "wealth" was compatible with the "rule of virtue" of Confucianism; the prosperity of the common people was an important manifestation of the "rule of virtue" of those in power. Of course, Confucius stressed wealth together with righteousness; one cannot seek wealth through unrighteous means or seek wealth which was forbidden. He said, "If wealth may be sought, I would be willing to be a gatekeeper at the market place to get it; if it cannot be sought, then I will do my own thing." ❹ He further said, "Wealth acquired unrighteously is just like a floating cloud as far as I am concerned." ❺ While others were seeking wealth, Confucius proposed the "Way" and "righteousness," in other words, the principles of reasonableness, fairness, and justice, which were the principles of moral ethics. Seeking wealth while maintaining righteousness was part of the moral orientation of Confucius. This was not only the view on profit that guided Confucius' actions, it was also the principle of universal value that Confucius felt would comfort the people. This was because when Confucius mentioned "wealth" and "profit," he was referring to them in the main in terms of the people, not the "wealth" and "profit" of the rulers garnered through over taxation; such "wealth" and "profit" were unrighteous.

As far as Confucius was concerned, those in government should not only enrich the people, but also respect them, and should not arbitrarily use them in hard labor for public works. He said, "Working the people in hard labor should be done just like performing a great sacrifice — very carefully, solemnly, and reverently." ❻ Those in government must have a profound understanding of the dignity, ambitions, and aspirations of the masses of the people; they must not merely regard them as the object of governing, and the tools for achieving

富足，国君哪会不足呢？百姓如果不足，国君怎么富足呢？"❶
有若所说，正体现了孔子德治惠民的思想。如何才能使百姓富裕
呢？孔子虽然很少谈到利，并反对"依据个人利益而行动"❷，
但是，他并不回避谈论"富"，认为追求富足是人之常情，他说：
"富与贵，是人的自然欲求。"❸ 因为在孔子看来，"富"与儒
家的"德治"是相通的，百姓富裕是政执者施行"德治"的重
要表现。当然，孔子强调的是富而有义，不可以追逐不义或不
可求的财富。他说："财富如果可以求得的话，就是做市场的
守门卒我也做；如果不可求，还是做我自己的事。"❹ 他还说：
"不义的富贵，在我看来，如同浮云一样。"❺ 孔子在人们追
求富贵之时，提出"道"与"义"，也就是合理、公平、公正
的原则，道德伦理的原则。求富贵而守义，这才是孔子的价值
取向。这既是孔子自己立身行事的义利观，也是孔子所认为的
具有普世价值的惠民原则，因为孔子所重视的"富"与"利"
主要是指"民"而言，不是统治者的"富"、"利"，统治者纳
税过度而"富"、"利"则不"义"。

在孔子看来，为政者不但应该富民，而且要敬民，不能随
意地役使民众。他说："役使百姓要像承当大祀典那样小心翼
翼，严肃恭敬。"❻ 为政者必须对民众的人格尊严、意志愿望
有深切的了解，不能仅仅将百姓当成统治的对象，实现政治目

❶ 见《论语·颜渊》。
❷ 见《论语·里仁》。
❸ 见《论语·里仁》。
❹ 见《论语·述而》。
❺ 见《论语·述而》。
❻ 见《论语·颜渊》。

❶ See "Yan Yuan," *Lunyu*.
❷ See "Liren," *Lunyu*.
❸ See "Liren," *Lunyu*.
❹ See "Shu'er," *Lunyu*.
❺ See "Shu'er," *Lunyu*.
❻ See "Yan Yuan," *Lunyu*.

political objectives. Even if someone was forced into conducting a war, Confucius advocated the need to first teach the people and then battle. He said, "The good guide teach the people for seven years, afterwards they will let the people go to battle." He further said, "To let people who have not been trained or guided go to battle, is to cruelly threaten their lives." ❶Confucius' idea about teaching the people before sending them to battle embodied respect for the lives of the people. What is even more worthy of notice is that what Confucius meant by "teaching the people" possibly meant letting the people understand warfare, thus making them the main element of a "righteous war." This meant that they were not merely the tools of the rulers to gain political benefits. The significance of this was, "teaching the people" then going to battle was not only a measure of respect for the people, but also simultaneously a measure of respect for their aspirations and political rights.

Confucius' moral thinking reveals the relationship between moral ethics and politics, affirming the restraining role of the cultivation of character exerted on political concepts. In a feudal society, the ruling lord possessed the ultimate authority. Strengthening moral cultivation that is at the base of "humane" rule plays a certain positive role in restraining the violent. However, virtue and politics, that is, the "inner sage" and the "outer king," are realms that belong to different ideological categories. "A moral entity" that possesses the virtue of "humaneness" is not necessarily "a political entity." Political entities in a feudal system, often for the sake of the benefit of the ruling group, are not necessarily all able to possess the virtue of "humaneness." Therefore, government by the authority of sages is the ideal form of government by Confucius as well as Confucians, which is a rather large difference from realistic governments. Despite all of this, Confucius' thinking on moral rule remains a valuable treasure within traditional political thought in China. It has a strong people-based orientation and humanistic coloration, which created an important influence on historical rulers. Simultaneously, given the current background, moral cultivation on the part of those in power and by the management level doubtlessly plays an important role regarding building a good social order and guaranteeing the running of an ideal government. This is an important part in the modern element of Confucian thought.

的的工具。即使是不得已而进行的战争，孔子也主张需要对民众教而后战，他说："善人教导人民七年以后，也能够让他们作战了。"又说："让没有受到训练和教导的民众去作战，这是残害生命。"❶ 孔子强调教而后可战，体现了对民众生命的尊重。更值得注意的是，孔子所谓的"教民"可能还指让民众了解战争的性质，使他们真正成为正义战争的主体，而不仅仅是统治者获取政治利益的工具。从这个意义上说，"教民"而战不但是对民众生命的尊重，同时也是对民众意志与政治权利的尊重。

孔子的德治思想揭示了道德伦理与政治之间的关系，肯定了人格修养对于统治者政治观念的制约作用。在封建社会中，君主具有至高无上的权力，强化统治者以"仁"为本的道德修养，对于限制统治者的暴政起到了一定的积极作用。但是，道德与政治，也就是"内圣"与"外王"分属于不同领域的意识形态。具备"仁"德的"道德主体"未必就是"政治主体"。封建时代的政治主体往往因为统治集团的利益，未必都能怀有"仁"德，因此，圣者为王仅是孔子以及儒家的理想政治，与现实政治还有相当大的差异。尽管如此，孔子的德治思想仍是中国传统政治思想中的宝贵财富，其强烈的民本色彩、人文色彩，不但对历代统治者产生了重要影响，同时，在现代背景之下，行政执法以及管理阶层的道德修养，对于建立良好的社会秩序，保证理想政治的实施，无疑具有重要的作用，这也是儒家思想具有现代性的重要内容之一。

❶ 见《论语·子路》。

❶ See "Zilu," *Lunyu*.

《论语集解》书影

Picture of the *Selected Illustration of the Analects*

十　"文质彬彬"——孔子的文艺观

Chapter X　" Culture and Nature" : Confucius'
View on Arts and Letters

Confucianism is the mainstay of Chinese traditional culture; its view on arts and letters is deeply embodied in China's ancient traditions concerning arts and letters. Confucius has determined the basic framework and theoretical orientation of the Confucian view on these topics.

First of all, Confucius emphasized the role of arts and letters. This was manifested in a concentrated manner in Confucius' disquisition on the relationship between "culture" and "nature." What Confucius said about "culture" and "nature" included both meaning and format, quality and coloration. Confucius said, "When nature surpasses culture, then one becomes rustic; when culture surpasses nature then one becomes pedantic. When culture and nature are equalized, then one becomes a gentleman." ❶ As for the so-called term "equalized," the ancients felt that culture and nature corresponded, and one needed each half of the equation. This passage says that if one's natural character exceeds the culture that one has acquired, then one would apear crude and rustic; but if one's acquired culture exceeds one's natural character, then one would be vain and empty. When such virtues of inner cultivation as humaneness, righteousness, and morality are coordinated with such outer forms as the rites, music, culture, only then does the character of a gentleman stabalize. Some have doubted the relationship between culture and nature, pointing out the quote, "The gentleman has the nature of one, and that is all; why does one need culture?" ❷ Confucius' student Zigong once defended Confucius' thought, saying that nature and culture formed one entity, and were of equal importance. It was like a leopard losing its fur, and there would be then no difference between it and a dog or a sheep. This means that whatever nature one possessed, then one required that same type of culture to coordinate with it. It is evident that in Confucius' thought, culture and nature complement each other. Of course, what Confucius meant by "culture" included a rich content, not only limited to writings, it also referred to contemporary rites, institutions, cultural records, etc. Confucius once said, developing cultural refinement by means of the rites and music would allow one to become a perfect person. It is evident that such institutions and fine arts as the "rites" and "music" both pertain to "culture." In terms of this significance, Confucius' disquisition on the "rites" is an important content of his view on arts and letters. Sometimes, what Confucius meant by "culture" included the path towards embodying the virtue of humaneness through study. For instance, Confucius' student Zigong asked him what did "culture" mean? Confucius replied, "To be quick and active, to love learning, yet to be humble enough to learn from interiors and not be ashamed, this is all culture." ❸

　　儒家作为中国传统文化的主干，其文艺观也深深地体现在中国古代文艺传统之中。孔子确定了儒家文艺观的基本构架与理论取向。

　　首先，孔子重视文艺的作用。这集中体现在孔子关于"文"与"质"的关系的论述中。孔子所说的"文"与"质"具有内容与形式、质朴与文彩的含义。孔子说："质胜文则野，文胜质则史。文质彬彬，然后君子。" ❶ 所谓"彬彬"，古人认为是文质相称，各得其半的样子。这段话是说，质朴多于文彩，就显得粗野；文彩多于质朴，则又流于虚浮。只有仁义道德等内在修养与礼乐文化等外在形式配合适当，才是君子的风格。有人对孔子所说的文质关系提出疑问，指出："君子质而已矣，何以文为？" ❷ 孔子的学生子贡对孔子的思想进行了辩护，他说，质与文互为一体，同等重要，就好像虎豹除去毛之后，便与狗、羊没有什么区别了。也就是说，有什么样的质，就需要什么样的文与其相配合。可见，文与质在孔子的思想中是相辅相成的。当然，孔子所说的"文"含有丰富的内容，不仅仅限于文章，还指当时的礼乐、制度、文化典籍等。孔子说过，以礼乐成就文采，就可以是完人了。可见，"礼"、"乐"等制度、艺术都属于"文"，从这个意义上说，孔子对于"礼"的论述，也是他的文艺观的重要内容。有时，孔子所说的"文"还包括通过学习而体现仁德的途径。如，孔子的学生子贡问孔子什么叫做"文"，孔子说："聪敏灵活，爱好学问，又谦虚下问，不以为耻，这就叫做文。" ❸

❶ 见《论语·雍也》。
❷ 见《论语·颜渊》。
❸ 见《论语·公冶长》。

❶ See "Yongye," *Lunyu*.
❷ See "Yan Yuan," *Lunyu*.
❸ See "Gongye Chang," *Lunyu*.

Confucius' view on arts and letters consisting of the unity between culture and nature was also an expression of his moral thinking. "Humaneness" and "rites" were the core fields of his thinking, and the relationship between them both influenced and restrained Confucius' view on arts and letters. In his view, the "rites" pertained to cultural refinement while "humaneness" pertained to nature; "humaneness" and the "rites" expressed an outer relationship of an inward unity. This type of relationship is expressed in the literary relationship between "culture" and "nature." While treating the relationship between virtue and arts and letters, Confucius said, "Set your resolve on the Way, base yourself on virtue, rely on humaneness, and explore freely on the arts." ❶ "Freely exploring on the arts" explains that the "arts" are part of the entire cultural tradition of the Way, virtue, and humaneness, etc. It is a type of artistic form pertaining to "humaneness," the highest moral ideals. Simultaneously, this artistic form also possesses the characteristic of "play," that is, "enjoyment." Of course, this type of entertainment process inevitably embodies the rich traces of the "Way," "virtue," and "humaneness." Therefore, Confucius' view on arts and letters was filled with a rich hue of morality. The *Analects* contains many examples of this. For example, when Confucius' student Zixia asked about the meaning of the line in the *Book of Poetry* that says "A beautiful smile and dimpled cheeks, the black and white of the eyes clearly demarked, flashing glances so fetching, and powder as background," Confucius said that it was describing the process of painting: First apply a background of white, then apply the patterns. Zixia intuitively grasped it, and said, "Is it therefore true that the creation of the rites and music comes later?" Confucius was delighted, and said, "Oh, Zixia, you are someone who can truly enlighten me! Now I can discuss the *Book of Poetry* with you." ❷ Although Zixia did not say what it was that "ritual" followed, Confucius was entirely satisfied with Zixia's answer. It is evident that both teacher and student understood each other intuitively; doubtlessly the foreground was the concept of "humanness" that they constantly discussed. In other words, it was similar to needing to first be humane, then engage in ritual; painting then first required a background of white be applied, then colors could be applied to paint a beautiful image. Zixia was quick and clever and earned Confucius' praise; this was due to his deep apprehension that the relationship between culture and nature in the thought of Confucius was the same with the relationship between humaneness and ritual.

Despite all of this, Confucius' view on culture and nature was basically to regard them with equal emphasis. Confucius also said the following in support of the importance of refinement, "An old record says, speech is sufficient to

孔子的文质统一的文艺观也是其伦理思想的体现。"仁"与"礼"是孔子思想的核心范畴,"仁"与"礼"的关系也影响并制约着孔子的文艺观。在孔子的文艺思想中,"礼"属于文彩,"仁"属于素质,"仁"与"礼"是一体共生的表里关系,这种关系表现在文艺上就是"文"与"质"的关系。孔子在处理道德与文艺之间的关系时说:"志于道,据于德,依于仁,游于艺。"❶"游于艺"说明了"艺"是道、德、仁等整个文化系统中的一个部分,是从属于最高道德理想"仁"的一种艺术形式。同时,这个艺术形式又具有"游戏"也就是娱乐的特征,当然,这种娱乐过程也必然带有浓厚的"道"、"德"、"仁"的痕迹。因此,孔子的文艺观充满着浓厚的道德色彩。对此,《论语》中不乏其例。如,当孔子的学生子夏问《诗经》中"巧笑倩兮,美目盼兮,素以为绚兮"是什么意思时,孔子说,这就好像作画,先画上白色的底子,然后再画上花。子夏心领神会,说:"是不是礼乐的产生在后呢?"孔子非常高兴,说:"子夏啊,你真是能启发我的人啊!现在我可以和你讨论《诗经》了。"❷虽然子夏没有回答"礼"在什么之后,但孔子对子夏的回答十分满意,可见,这一定是他们师生心领神会的内容,无疑是指他们经常讨论的"仁"。也就是说,就像先仁而后礼一样,绘画也要先打好白色的底子,然后再绘五彩,画上美艳的图像。子夏机敏而得到孔子的赞赏,就是因为他深切地领会了孔子思想中文与质的关系即如同仁与礼的关系一样。

尽管如此,孔子的文质观基本还是以文质并重为主。孔子还说过这样重视文彩的话:"志有之:言以足志,文以足言;不言,

❶《论语·述而》。
❷ 见《论语·八佾》。

❶ "Shu'er," *Lunyu*.
❷ See "Bayi," *Lunyu*.

express the resolve, and literary embellishment is sufficient to express speech. But if one does not speak, then who will learn of one's resolve? Language without literary embellishment will not circulate very far." ❶ This means that without the expression of language, how can one learn of another's "resolve" ? But without the coloration of style, such language would not circulate very far or wide. It is evident that culture and nature benefit and enhance each other, which is the fundamental orientation of Confucius' view on culture and nature. What must be pointed out is, paying equal emphasis to both culture and nature of Confucius and the Confucians was not very evident before the Qin Dynasty. This viewpoint was already criticized by the Legalists. Han Feizi said that the Confucians "confused the law with their literary rhetoric." ❷ The unified view on culture and nature of Confucius has exerted an important influence on ancient aesthetics in China as well as on arts and letters.

Next is about Confucius' view on poetry. In his approach to arts and letters, Confucius heavily emphasized poetry. His rather rich theories of poetry established the foundation of poetics of Confucianism, influencing the fundamental orientation of the development of classical poetry in China. Confucius' view on poetry was the core of his thought on arts and letters, and was an important component of his entire system of thought. Concerning the position of poetry within arts and letters, Confucius in the main stressed the educative role of poetry. Confucius said, "Be inspired by the poems, be established by the rites, and be completed by music." ❸ This means that poetry provides spiritual encouragement, ritual establishes one in society, and music and dance complete this process. The formation of ritual needs to be achieved through the roles played by poetry and music. Poetry is the necessary condition for self-cultivation, for poetry easily arouses the emotions, arousing the yearnings of the people to move forwards towards goodness and to abandon evil. Therefore, Confucius regarded poetry first of all as an important method of moral cultivation. Education in poetry and education in ritual formed a single entity, with poetry occupying the leading position. As far as Confucius was concerned, poetry could express the emotions; and the recitation of poetry could inspire the heart, encourage people to progress, and thereby produce the function of cultivating the person and establishing virtue. This is what he meant by "being inspired by poetry." "Being established by the rites" means one must first study the rites before taking one's place in society. After "being established by the rites" one's personal moral cultivation has not yet been completed; it is still necessary to "be completed by music," which means to cultivate the nature and emotions through music. Only then can one perfect one's virtue. Confucius

谁知其志！言之无文，行而不远。"❶ 就是说，没有语言表达，哪里能知道"志"呢？语言没有文彩，流传也不会广泛久远。可见，文质相得益彰，是孔子文质观的基本取向。需要指出的是，孔子以及儒家文质兼重的观念在秦代以前并不多见，这一观念曾经受到法家的批评，韩非说儒家"以文乱法"❷。孔子文质统一的观念，对于中国古代美学以及文艺传统产生了重要的影响。

其次，孔子对于诗歌的论述。在种种文艺样式之中，孔子十分重视诗歌。他较丰富的诗论奠定了儒家诗学的基础，影响了中国古典诗歌发展的基本走向。孔子的诗论是其文艺思想的核心，也是其整个思想体系中的重要组成部分。对于诗歌在文艺中的地位，孔子主要是从教化的功能来认识的。孔子说："兴于诗，立于礼，成于乐。"❸ 意思是说，诗歌给人以精神鼓励，礼使人立于世，而音乐、舞蹈则使这一过程得以完成。礼的形成，需通过诗、乐的作用得以实现。诗歌是修身的必要条件，诗歌易于唤起情感，唤起人们对善的向往，对恶的扬弃，因此，孔子将诗歌首先看作是修养德性的重要手段，诗歌教育与礼乐教育形成了一个整体，而以诗歌教育居于首位。在孔子看来，诗歌可以抒发感情，朗诵诗歌，可以振奋人心，勉力进取，从而产生修身立德的功能，这就是他所说的"兴于诗"。"立于礼"，是说学礼才能立身。"立于礼"之后，人的道德修养并未完成，还需"成于乐"，就是通过音乐来修养性情，最

❶《左传·襄公二十五年》。
❷《论语·泰伯》。
❸《韩非子·五蠹》。

❶ "Duke Xiang 25th year," *Zuozhuan*.
❷ "Taibo," *Lunyu*.
❸ "Wudu," *Han Feizi*.

regarded poetry, ritual, and music that are connected together as the three essential components of self-cultivation. Poetry, ritual, and music are all methods of and paths towards moral cultivation; moral cultivation then is the fundamental goal. In this regard, ancient Chinese sources have clearly expressed this thinking of Confucius: "Where the intention goes, there also goes poetry; wherever poetry goes, there too goes ritual. Wherever ritual goes, there too goes music." ❶ This means that wherever the goal of moral cultivation goes, poetry also goes there; wherever poetry goes, then ritual goes there; wherever ritual goes, then music goes there too. It is evident that the relationship between "poetry," "ritual," and "music" and the "intention" of moral cultivation is a relationship between method and goal. Poetry, music, and dance, all as aspects of "art," anciently formed a trinity. Confucians felt that poetry was the core of this trio, for both music and dance pertained to and expressed poetry. To understand Confucius' thinking on poetics is to grasp the core and substance of Confucius' thinking on arts and letters.

As for the social function of poetry, Confucius developed an even more systematic disquisition. He once sighed, "Why don't you study poetry, young one? It can inspire, give you new viewpoints, let you harmonize, and let you express resentment. Close at hand, serve one's father; further off serve one's lord. Learn much of the names of birds, beasts, plants, and trees." ❷ "Inspiration," "viewpoints," "harmonizing," and "resentment" are all simple summaries of Confucius' views on the social role of poetry. "Inspiration" means that poetry can arouse the emotions and imaginations of people. "Viewpoints" means that poetry possesses the function of knowledge, and that through poetry one can see the flourishing or decay of social mores and political gains and losses. Poetry also reflects social life and human and non-human entities. "Harmonizing" indicates that poetry can coordinate emotions and promote the blending of different feelings. "Resentment" means that poetry can vent the dissatisfaction of the mass of the people, express emotions, and play a certain role in the clearing out of feelings. Poetry can not only exert the function of criticizing reality, but also prevent the intensification of contradictions within society. Of course, the content of "resentment" within poetry that Confucius discussed was not limited to the satire of society or criticism of politics; family, friends, the complex feelings in male and female relations—all can be expressed through poetry. "Close at hand, serve one's father; further off serve one's lord. Learn much of the names of birds, beasts, plants, and trees" —this mentions how poetry can

终成就完善的品德。孔子将诗、礼、乐当作互相联系的修身三要素，诗、礼、乐都是道德修养的方法与途径，道德修养是根本目的。对此，中国古代文献中曾明确地表现孔子的这一思想："志之所至，诗亦至焉；诗之所至，礼亦至焉；礼之所至，乐亦至焉。" ❶ 就是说，道德修养的目的在哪里，诗就到哪里；诗到哪里，礼就到哪里；礼到哪里，乐就到了哪里。可见，"诗"、"礼"、"乐"与道德修养之"志"的关系是手段与目的的关系。同为"艺"的诗、乐、舞在古代是三位一体的，儒家认为诗是三者中的核心，乐、舞都是从属于诗歌、表现诗歌的。理解了孔子的诗学思想，也就把握了孔子文艺思想的核心与本质。

对于诗歌的社会功能，孔子还有更为系统的论述。他感叹道："小子何莫学夫诗？诗，可以兴，可以观，可以群，可以怨。迩之事父，远之事君；多识于鸟兽草木之名。" ❷ "兴"、"观"、"群"、"怨"是孔子对于诗歌社会作用的简明概括。"兴"，是指诗歌可以激发人们的情感与想象。"观"，是指诗歌具有认识的作用，通过诗歌可以见风俗的盛衰、政治的得失，诗歌可以反映社会生活以及人情物态。"群"，是指诗歌可以协调情感，促进感情融合。"怨"，是指诗歌可以表达民众的不满，宣泄情感，对政治起到一定的疏导作用，诗歌既可以具有批判现实的作用，也可以防止社会矛盾的激化。当然，孔子所论的诗歌"怨"的内容，并不限于社会政治的讽刺与批评，家庭、朋友、男女之间郁结的情感，都可以借诗歌来抒发。"迩之事父，远之事君，多识于鸟兽草木之名"，是说诗歌承担着政治、伦理

❶《礼记·孔子闲居》。
❷《论语·阳货》。

❶ "Confucius xianju," *Liji.*
❷ "Yang Huo," *Lunyu.*

assume the roles of spreading political and ethical teachings and of the transmission of knowledge. Confucius' knowledge of the functions of poetry systematically embodied the functions of such aspects as the expression of feelings, artistic effect, as well as social knowledge.

Confucius held to another rather aggressive theory concerning the role of poetry. He felt that poetry played a unique role in the life of the people. Once Confucius asked Kong Li whether he had studied the "Zhounan" and "Shaonan" sections of the *Book of Poetry*. Confucius also stated, "If one does not learn the 'Zhounan' and 'Shaonan,' wouldn't it be just like standing facing a wall?" ❶ This means that if one does not research the "Zhounan" and "Shaonan," then it would be similar to standing with one's face towards the wall; not knowing these sections of the *Book of Poetry* would be like being unable to see anything or not being able to take a single step forward. He even stated, "If you do not study poetry then you won't be able to talk." ❷ What Confucius emphasized concerning poetry was its effect on society, only then came its appreciation. If what one learned from poetry was not applied, then one did not reach the goal of studying poetry in the first place. He said, "As for the *Book of Poetry*, if taught to an official and he cannot apply them, and if you then send him out to the four quarters but he cannot respond on his own. Then why do it?" ❸ This means that when somebody has thoroughly mastered the *Book of Poetry* and then he is assigned some administrative task but he is unable to handle it, or when dispatching him on a diplomatic mission, he is not able to respond freely in his negotiations. Then of what use is his learning of all these poems? It is evident that Confucius' first demand in learning the poems is their function in society, especially their political function. Confucius' stress on the social function of poetry is directly related to the popular practice of "citing poetry" during the Spring and Autumn Period. According to the historical records, ancient arena of diplomacy often witnessed the quotation of poetry or the composition of a poem as a way to make a response; this allowed for the use of the pleasing language of poetry to make a tactful advocacy of one's position. It is evident that poetry was an artistic form intimately tied to social life.

On the surface it seems that Confucius seldom discussed the artistic forms of poetry since he stressed its utility and application. Actually, when he said "If you do not study poetry then you won't be able to talk," it was precisely an expression of his veneration of the artistry and verbal skill involved in poetry. Confucius demanded that poetic language be used to reflect life, which precisely expressed his lofty demand concerning artistic

的教化功能和知识传播的作用。孔子对于诗歌功能的认识，系统地体现了诗歌具有的情感抒发、艺术感染以及社会认识等方面的作用。

孔子对于诗歌的作用还有较为激进的论述，他认为诗歌在人们的生活中具有不可替代的作用。他曾问孔鲤是否研究过《诗经》中的《周南》、《召南》，并且说："人而不为《周南》、《召南》，其犹正墙面而立也与？"❶ 意思是说，人如果不研究《周南》、《召南》，那会像面对墙壁而站着；不知《周南》、《召南》，就如同一物不能见，一步不能行一样。他甚至说"不学诗就不会说话"❷。孔子对于诗歌首先重视的是社会效用，其次才是欣赏。如果学诗而不致用，则不能达到学诗的目的。他说："诵《诗三百》，授之以政，不达；使于四方，不能专对；虽多，亦奚以为？"❸意思是说，熟读《诗经》，交给他行政的任务却办不通；让他出使外国，又不能应对自如。虽然读诗很多，又有什么用呢？可见，他是以社会功能，尤其是诗歌的政治功能为第一要求。孔子对诗歌社会功能的强调，与春秋时期盛行的"称诗"现象有直接的关系。据史书记载，古代外交场合常常是引诗或作诗对答，以含蓄的诗性语言表达主张。可见，诗歌是与社会生活息息相关的艺术形式。

表面看来，孔子论诗重致用、重功能，而很少有对诗歌艺术形式的讨论，其实，孔子说"不学诗无以言"，正是崇尚艺术、崇尚文彩的表现。孔子要求以诗性的语言反映生活，正体现了孔子对艺术形式有很高的要求，他所说的"言之无文，行而不

❶《论语·阳货》。
❷ 见《论语·季氏》。
❸《论语·子路》。

❶ "Yang Huo," *Lunyu*.
❷ See "Jishi," *Lunyu*.
❸ "Zilu," *Lunyu*.

form. What he said concerning "Language without literary embellishment will not circulate very far," ❶ should in the main refer to poetry. Therefore, Confucius' thought on poetics similarly placed equal weight on culture and nature, that is to say, content and format are unified. Confucius' disquisitions on poetics created a profound effect on the formation of the study of poetry in ancient China and on the historical development of education as well as literature. The long history of Chinese civilization enjoys a rich coloration of poetry, and has to be related to the great role played by what Confucius, who said about "language without literary embellishment will not circulate very far" and about "inspiration," "viewpoints," "harmonizing," and "resentment."

Finally, let's discuss Confucius' understanding of music. In the ancient time, poetry and music were equivalent; Confucius regarded poetry and music as important educational tools, and hence highly emphasized music. Confucius once studied music with a renowned musician, and once told the master of music in the state of Lu about the Way of music: "Music is something that can be understood: At the beginning of the performance it should be played allegro with energy; as it proceeds it should be played andante and harmonize all the parts, orderly and clearly. It should be drawn out continuously, and finally reach the grand coda with all parts played in unison." ❷ He used simple phrases to describe the characteristics of each segment of the music. Confucius also knew how to appreciate music. When he was in the state of Qi and heard "Shao" music, he was so deeply attracted by it that for three months he did not notice the taste of meat. He sighed, saying, "Who would have thought that the enjoyment of music could reach such sublime heights!" ❸ He had a profound understanding of music, and was able to intuit the composer and the emotions that was expressing through music. Additionally, Confucius was also good at singing. When he sang with others, if the song was moving, he would ask the other fellow to sing it again alone, then he would join in and sing it again. He certainly was mesmerized by music! The *Analects* records that if Confucius cried because of some reason, he would not sing that day; from this we can perceive that Confucius sang constantly. The aspirations of Confucius' student Zeng Dian were different from those of his other fellow students. What Zeng Dian wanted to do was to go with adults and children to bathe in the waters at Yi during the third month of late spring; there they would take in the breeze on the Wuyu Terrace, and then return singing on the way. Confucius approved and identified with Zeng Dian's life of song with all his heart. It is evident that Confucius deeply loved music and was well versed in it. Confucius not only "freely explored the arts," but also integrated music and song together with

远" ❶应该主要是指诗歌而言。因此，孔子的诗学思想同样体现了文质并重，也就是内容与形式相统一的特征。孔子的诗论对中国古代诗学传统的形成，对中国历代教育和文学都产生了深刻的影响。悠久的中华文明带有浓郁的诗性色彩，这与孔子提出"不学诗无以言"以及诗歌具有"兴、观、群、怨"的巨大功能不无关系。

最后，孔子对音乐的认识。古代诗乐互通，孔子将诗、乐看成是教化的重要手段，对音乐也十分重视。孔子曾向著名的乐工学习音乐，他将演奏音乐的道理告诉鲁国的太师，说："音乐是可以理解的：开始演奏时激昂热烈，继而舒缓和谐，条理清晰，绵绵不绝，最后再合而成之。" ❷以简明的语言描述了音乐几个部分的特点。孔子还很会欣赏音乐，他在齐国听到《韶》乐时，深深地被其吸引，竟然三个月尝不出肉的味道，感叹道："想不到欣赏音乐竟达到如此境界。" ❸他对音乐有很深的理解，能够通过音乐体悟出作者及其所表达的情感。不但如此，孔子还善于歌唱，他与别人一起唱歌，如果歌曲动听，他一定请别人再唱一遍，然后自己和唱一遍，为音乐的魅力所陶醉。《论语》中记载，孔子如果因事而流泪，这一天就不唱歌，由此可见孔子是经常唱歌的。他的学生曾点的志向与其他同学不同，曾点向往的是暮春三月，与大人孩子一起在沂水中沐浴，迎风站立在舞雩台上，最后一起歌唱而归。孔子由衷地赞叹与认同曾点的歌咏人生。可见，孔子深爱且深谙音乐。孔子不但"游于艺"，还将音乐与诗歌、礼仪结合在一起，并由此体现他的政治观、伦理观与人性

❶《左传·襄公二十五年》。
❷ 见《论语·八佾》。
❸ 见《论语·述而》。

❶ "Duke Xiang 25th year," *Zuozhuan*.
❷ See "Bayi," *Lunyu*.
❸ See "Shu'er," *Lunyu*.

rituals and ceremonies, which embodied his political, ethical view, and view on human life. Just as the American scholar Fingarette said:

> Over the long run I have been deeply impressed reading about Confucius' love of music and the fundamental significance of his humanism and value system that are infused with music; in my view, many of Confucius' conceptual ideals and profound insight are easily elucidated through analogies with music (in reference to the *Analects*, "Taibo," verse eight: "Be inspired by the poems, be established by the rites, and be completed by music."). This is not just an accidental occurrence. When Confucius pondered over his ideals, he expressed his thought through the medium of music. ❶

Confucius' understanding of music, up to the point of being able to "use the form of music to engage in thinking," was due to his deep recognition of the function of music in education and of the characteristics of its aesthetics. Confucius proposed the integration of goodness and beauty as the most sublime aesthetic realm of music, based on utilizing in music the conceptions of humanness and ritual that pertained to moral philosophy, and the culture and nature of an artistic conception. When Confucius was discussing how to govern a state with Yan Yuan, he said, "Use the calendar system of the Xia Dynasty, ride in carriages of the Yin Dynasty, wear the ritual caps of the Zhou Dynasty, and as for music, use 'Shao and Wu.' " ❷ Scholars of the Han Dynasty interpreted the so-called "Shao and Wu" as the "Shao" and "Wu" music from the time of Shun. Confucius once compared "Shao" and "Wu" music, concluding that "Shao" music was the ultimate in beauty, as well as the ultimate in goodness. As for "Wu," it was also the ultimate in beauty but did not express enough goodness. As for this viewpoint of Confucius, scholars of later generations supposed that "Shao" music praised Shun because of his moral conduct that brought universal peace to the world. Although King Wu of Zhou had the merit of establishing a dynasty, still his use of military force destroyed the Shang Dynasty; therefore "Wu" music could not completely express goodness. It is evident that Confucius demanded music of not only beauty of form, but beauty of content as well. The human character manifested by music is that of the inner moral character; only with this can one arrive at the realm of the ultimate in goodness and in beauty, thus arriving at the lofty unity of form and content. As far as concrete music goes, classical "Shao" music was the true classical and pure music, and was the "orthodox sounds" promoted by Confucius. But Confucius detested the music of the state of

观。正如美国学者芬格莱特所说：

> 长期以来，对于孔子热爱音乐并赋予音乐以人性的基本意义和价值这一事实，我一直印象颇深。在我看来，孔子许多关键的理念和睿识洞见能够很容易地通过音乐的类比来加以阐明（是指《论语·泰伯篇第八》："兴于诗，立于礼，成于乐。"），这决不是偶然的巧合。当孔子思考他的理想时，他是以音乐的方式来进行思考的。❶

孔子理解音乐，乃至"用音乐的方式来进行思考"，是由于他对音乐的教化功能、审美特征有深刻的认识。孔子将道德哲学的仁与礼、文艺观念的文与质运用于音乐，提出善与美的结合是音乐的最佳审美境界。孔子在与颜渊讨论怎样治理国家时说："用夏代的历法，坐殷朝的车子，戴周朝的礼帽，音乐则用《韶舞》。"❷ 所谓《韶舞》，汉代学者认为就是舜时的音乐《韶》与《武》。孔子曾将《韶》乐与《武》乐作比较，认为《韶》美极了，并且好极了；论到《武》，则说美极了，但还不够好。对于孔子的这一看法，后世的学者认为：《韶》乐赞美舜因德行而使天下太平；周武王虽有功业，但是用武力消灭商朝，因此《武》乐便未能尽善。可见，孔子对于音乐不但要求形式之美，还要求内容之善。音乐所表现的人物有内在的德行，才有可能达到尽善尽美的境界，达到内容与形式的高度统一。就具体的音乐而言，古典的《韶》乐是典雅纯正的音乐，是孔子推崇的"正声"。孔子对于当时流行

❶ 见《孔子：即凡而圣》，第101页。
❷ 见《论语·卫灵公》。

❶ See *Confucius: The Secular as Sacred*, p. 101.
❷ See "Weilinggong," *Lunyu*.

Zheng, the popular music of the day (the "sound of Zheng"); he felt that "Zheng music was depraved." ❶ He "detested that the sound of Zheng destroyed classical music." ❷ "Xianjin" in the *Analects* records the following incident. Confucius' student Zilu was playing the *qin*; but Confucius, who normally loved music, was not pleased, so his students were not very respectful of Zilu. Why did Zilu make Confucius angry? It was because what Zilu was playing was a tune that partook of the "sound of the northern borders," and the "sound of killing and conquest." This is to say, the music of the far northern border country represented the music of warfare, not the classical and pure music that was compatible with ritual which Confucius venerated. Therefore, it was not strange that Zilu was criticized. Confucius adopted different attitudes towards different music; the reason for this was that he regarded ritual and music as integrated with ethics and politics, and that ritual and music embodied the methods of ethics and politics. He said, "When the Way prevails in the world, the devising of rituals and music and the calling forth of the army are all matters decided by the son of heaven; but when the Way is lacking, all these are decided by the feudal princes." ❸ The music from the son of heaven was also distinguished by being music of the Way; the music of the feudal princes was music without the Way. Music is also the manifestation and the embodiment of a moral government. Confucius felt that music should be blended together with ritual, and musical performance should conform to the standards of rites and ceremonies. When Confucius observed a grandee of Lu, the head of the Ji clan, watching a performance of a dance with 64 dancers, which should have been reserved for the son of heaven, he became thoroughly enraged, and said, "If this can be endured, what can't be endured?" ❹ Such actions that exceeded the bounds of ritual propriety, in the view of Confucius, were due to the behavior of the lord in not cultivating his virtue. He said, "If a person does not have the virtue of humaneness, how can he handle the system of rites and music?" ❺ It is evident that Confucius' theory of music contained a rich coloration of morality; it likewise embodied the unification of "culture" and "nature."

Confucius' thought on arts and letters is connected with such moral and ethical conceptions as "humaneness" and "ritual." This not only expresses the

的郑国的音乐（"郑声"）则十分厌恶，认为"郑声淫❶，他"憎恶郑声破坏了典雅的音乐"。❷在《论语·先进篇》中还记载了这样一件事，孔子的学生子路弹奏乐曲，但喜欢音乐的孔子却并不高兴，学生们因此对子路便不太恭敬。子路为何引起孔子的不快？这是因为子路所弹的曲调有"北鄙之声"、"杀伐之声"，也就是北方边远地区表现战争的乐曲，不是孔子所崇尚的合礼的典雅纯正音乐，因此，受到孔子的异议就不足为怪了。孔子对于不同的"乐"采取不同的态度，原因就是他认为礼乐是与伦理、政治结合在一起的，礼乐是体现伦理、政治的手段，他说："天下有道，制礼作乐以及出兵都决定于天子；天下无道，制礼作乐以及出兵便决定于诸侯。"❸出自天子与诸侯的音乐也有"有道"与"无道"之别，音乐也是道德政治的体现与载体。孔子认为音乐应该与礼融合在一起，音乐表演应该符合礼仪规范，孔子看到鲁国的大夫季氏居然演奏天子所用的六十四人的舞乐时，十分气愤地说："如果这都能容忍，还有什么不可容忍的呢？"❹这些越礼的行为，在孔子看来，是因为主人不修仁德的结果，孔子说："人如果没有仁德，怎样来对待礼乐制度呢？"❺可见，孔子论乐同样带有浓厚的道德色彩，同样主张"文"与"质"相统一。

孔子的文艺思想是与"仁"、"礼"等道德伦理观念相联系的，这既表现为文、质之间的和谐统一，也要求在艺术表现方

❶ 见《论语·卫灵公》。
❷ 见《论语·阳货》。
❸ 见《论语·季氏》。
❹ 见《论语·八佾》。
❺ 见《论语·八佾》。

❶ See "Weilinggong," *Lunyu*.
❷ See "Yang Huo," *Lunyu*.
❸ See "Jishi," *Lunyu*.
❹ See "Bayi," *Lunyu*.
❺ See "Bayi," *Lunyu*.

harmony and unity between culture and nature, but also demands that the performance of fine arts be happy without being excessive, sorrowful without being wounded, resentful without being enraged. The "poetics" of later generations that evolved into "gentleness and kindness" precisely has inherited the orientation of Confucius' aesthetics. The Confucian view on arts and letters that Confucius inaugurates profoundly influences on Chinese classical literature and fine arts, forming the fundamental paradigm of arts and letters in ancient China.

面做到快乐而不过分，悲哀而不伤恸，幽怨而不愤怒。后代推演出的"温柔敦厚"的"诗教"正继承了孔子的审美取向。孔子开启的儒家文艺观，深深地影响了中国古典文学与艺术，形成了中国古代文艺的基本框架。

历代绘画中不同的孔子形象

Images of Confucius in paintings of different periods

十一　泽溉中华　惠及寰宇
——孔子的文化影响

Chapter XI　Pervading China, and Blessing the
World: The Cultural Influence of
Confucius

While young, Confucius became famous on the basis of his knowledge of the rites. Later, he traveled among various states, accepting students from all regions; his learning and thought was thereby promulgated on a broad scale, and he established the scholarly Confucian School. Through the reception, development, and transmission by later scholars, the culture of the Confucian School formed the core of Chinese culture, and Confucius became the most outstanding representative of this Chinese culture. Following the broad promulgation of Confucianism throughout East and Southeast Asia, Confucianism now has become an important aspect of the diverse modern world culture, and more importantly, Confucius has become the symbol of Eastern culture and, by common consent, a great man within world culture. What is worth noticing is that, although Confucius was the founder of Confucianism, still the study of Confucius is not entirely the same as the study of Confucianism. This is because often later Confucian scholars cited his recorded conversations to construct new scholarly theories, even to the extent of incorporating cultural elements from Buddhism or Daoism. Therefore, Confucian learning in later generations is called the "Neo-Confucianism." Despite all this, the fundamental value system of Confucianism derived from Confucius. The transformation and development of Confucianism actually has already started after the death of Confucius. It is precisely this type of development and transformation that enables this mainstream current of traditional Chinese culture to be able to remain vital and growing, and exert an obvious and unique attraction within the diverse world culture.

First is about the influence of later scholarship on the dissemination and development of Confucianism. In addition to the attractiveness of his own theories, Confucius' thought is able to exert a huge influence because of the dissemination and development of his disciples. Throughout his entire life, Confucius recruited and accepted a vast number of disciples; according to historical records, there were around 3,000 of his followers and 72 persons among them had personally mastered the "Six Arts." They played a great role in the dissemination of Confucius' thought. After Confucius died, his disciples dispersed throughout the various states of the feudal lords, and spread his thought throughout every level of society. Among his disciples, some became the teachers or friends of the upper class aristocrats, accelerating and broadening the influence of Confucian learning. The understanding of these disciples of Confucian learning contained differences, thus forming different schools; together they constituted the model for early Confucianism. According to early accounts, after Confucius, Confucianism divided into the following

孔子早年即以知礼著称，其后周游列国，广收门徒，学问思想得到了广泛的传播，并创立了儒家学派。经过后代学者的继承、发展与传播，儒家文化成了中国文化的核心，孔子也成为中国文化最杰出的代表。随着儒学在东亚、东南亚的广泛传播，儒学已成为当今世界多元文化中的一个重要方面，孔子更成为东方文化的象征和公认的世界文化伟人。值得注意的是，孔子虽然是儒学的创始人，但孔学并不完全等同于儒学，这是因为后世的儒者往往引孔子的语录而构建新的学说，甚至吸取佛教、道教的文化因素，于是后世的儒学又被称为"新儒学"。尽管如此，儒学的基本价值观念还是来源于孔子。儒学的变化与发展其实从孔子去世之后就已开始。正是这种发展与变化，才使得作为中国传统文化主流的儒学能够生生不息，在世界多元文化之中彰显独特的魅力。

一、孔门后学对儒学的传播与发展。孔子思想能够产生巨大的影响，除了本身的理论魅力之外，还在于孔门弟子的传播与发展。孔子一生招收弟子众多，据史书记载，孔子的门人大概有三千人，其中身通"六艺"的有七十二人，他们对孔子思想的传播产生了巨大的作用。孔子去世后，弟子们散居在各诸侯国，在各个阶层传播孔子思想，其中有些成为上层贵族的老师与朋友，使儒学的影响迅速扩大。弟子们对孔学的理解也有差异，于是形成了不同的派别，他们共同形成了早期儒学的规模。据文献记载，孔子之后，儒家分为八派，分别是：子张之

eight schools: that of Zizhang, that of Zisi, that of Mr. Yan, that of Mr. Meng, that of Mr. Qidiao, that of Mr. Zhongliang, that of Mr. Sun, and that of Mr. Yuezheng. That the disciples divided into different branches actually had a certain relationship with the development of Confucius' own thought; the time when these disciples began their studies and the content of their studies all differed. Disciples of the early period such as Zixia and Ziyou in the main studied ritual and music with Confucius, and were not able to systematically study the mature thought of the master, especially that of "humaneness." Disciples of the late period such as Zengzi and Zizhang et al. were taught the thought of Confucius' mature period. Therefore, the understanding and interpretation of the disciples in the Confucian schools were different, and naturally formed different schools; this was unavoidable. Here let us briefly introduce those outstanding disciples and second-generation disciples, who disseminated Confucius' thought.

Zixia promulgated Confucianism in the state of Wei. After Confucius died, his disciples scattered to various lands and disseminated Confucianism. Zilu was in the state of Wei, Zizhang was in Chen, Tantai Ziyu was in Chu, and Zigong was in Qi; the one with rather obvious results in promulgating these teaching was Zixia. According to historical records, among contemporary feudal lords, Marquis Wen of Wei was particularly fond of learning. Zixia and those who studied with him, Tianzi Fang, Duangan Mu, Wu Qi, and Qin Huali had all served as teachers of Marquis Wen, who established the office of academician to promote the study of Confucianism. Although there is no record of Zixia among the eight schools mentioned in *Han Feizi*, according to extant Confucian accounts, not only did Zixia foster the broad dissemination of Confucianism in the state of Wei, at the same time he also contributed greatly to the theoretical exposition of Confucian literature. Scholars of the Han Dynasty supposed that even though Confucius established such classics as the *Book of Poetry*, the *Book of Documents*, the *Rites*, and the *Book of Music*, the exposition of the contents of the Confucian classics was started by Zixia.

Zengzi disseminated the way of "filial piety." Confucius' theory is based on "humaneness," and "humanenss" is based on the thought of "loving one's family was the most important thing." ❶ Therefore, "filial piety," respect for the older generation, is the starting point of "humaneness." The concept of "filial piety" occupies an important position in Confucius' intellectual thought. A disciple of Confucius, late period, Zeng Shen (Zengzi), played an important role in inheriting and transmitting the way of

儒、子思之儒、颜氏之儒、孟氏之儒、漆雕氏之儒、仲良氏之儒、孙氏之儒、乐正氏之儒。孔子的弟子分为不同的流派其实与孔子本身的思想发展具有一定的关系，先后入门的弟子，学习的内容也不尽相同。如子夏、子游是早期弟子，主要从孔子学习礼乐，没有能够系统地学习孔子成熟期尤其是"仁"学思想，而晚期弟子如曾子、子张等继承的主要是孔子成熟时期的思想，因此，孔门弟子对于孔子思想的理解、解释也不尽相同，分成不同的流派也就在所难免。这里我们将传播孔子思想较突出的弟子及再传弟子略作介绍。

子夏在魏国传播儒学。孔子去世后，弟子们在各地传播儒学，子路在卫国，子张在陈国，澹台子羽在楚国，子贡在齐国，而传播效果尤其显著的则是子夏。据记载，当时的诸侯中魏文侯特别好学，子夏以及跟从子夏学习的田子方、段干木、吴起、禽滑厘等人都曾做过魏文侯的老师。魏文侯专门设置博士官提倡儒学。虽然《韩非子》记载的"儒分为八"中没有提到子夏，但从现存的文献看，子夏不但使儒学在魏国首先获得了广泛传播，同时还对儒家文献的理论阐发多有贡献。汉代人认为，儒家的《诗》、《书》、《礼》、《乐》等经书虽然由孔子确定，但是阐发儒家经典的内涵，则是从子夏开始的。

曾子传播"孝"道。孔子的学说以"仁"为本，而"仁"又以"爱自己的亲人最为重要"❶。因此，对长辈恭敬的"孝"是"仁"的起点，"孝"的观念在孔子学术思想中占据重要的地位。孔子晚年的弟子曾参（即曾子）对孔子孝道的继承与传

❶ 见《礼记·中庸》。

❶ See "Zhongyong," *Liji.*

filial piety of Confucius. In the ancient source *Da Dai Li Ji*, there are such chapters as "Zengzi Establishes Affairs," "Zengzi Grounds Filial Piety," "Zengzi Establishes Filial Piety," "Zengzi's Great Filiality," and "Zengzi Serves His Parents," etc. It is evident from these chapters that his role in spreading the way of filial piety of Confucius was particularly important. Such scholars as Liu Zongyuan of the Tang Dynasty and Cheng Yi of the Song Dynasty supposed that the *Analects* was written by Zengzi's disciples. Zengzi was Confucius' student during the late period, so he had a comprehensive understanding of Confucius' entire thought. Therefore, when answering Confucius, only Zengzi was able to explain the way of a "single thread" in Confucius' thought; he was obviously different from those students limited to conversing on views of the rites and music.

The following is about the influence of the schools of Zisi and Simeng on the reception and expansion of Confucius' thought. Zisi was not only Confucius' grandson, but also a second-generation disciple. Han Yu, the scholar of the Tang Dynasty, supposed that Zisi's learning derived from Zengzi. The renowned historian of the Han Dynasty Sima Qian supposed that Zisi created an important work of Confucianism, the *Doctrine of the Mean*, but this theory was doubted by later scholars. But the *Doctrine of the Mean* at least preserves the thought of Zisi. The *Doctrine of the Mean* was highly regarded by later generations of Confucians, and was considered to be "the transmission of the heart of the Confucian school" ; that is, it was a work that transmitted the ultimate core of the thought of Confucius. Confucian scholars of the Song Dynasty even selected the *Doctrine of the Mean*, the *Great Learning*, the *Analects*, and the *Mencius* to form the "Four Books," becoming the most important classic works and the main source of theory, which exerted a profound influence on the development of Chinese culture.

The importance of Zisi's theories is also evident in the inspiration that they provided for Mencius, who is representative of orthodox Confucianism. Xunzi, a thinker of the Warring States, considered that Mencius was a thinker who was responding to Zisi. The *Mencius* mentioned Zengzi and Zisi multiple times. The traditional line of succession from Confucius to Zengzi to Zisi and finally to Mencius, has gained broad consensus of later generations of scholars. Mencius was an important thinker in the Warring States, who developed the thought of Confucius in a comprehensive manner, and who was an important representative of Confucianism in the period of post-Confucius to pre-Qin period. The theory of the goodness of human nature that he proposed perfected the theoretical thought of Confucius; the humane governance that he

播起到了重要作用。中国古代文献《大戴礼记》中就有《曾子立事》、《曾子本孝》、《曾子立孝》、《曾子大孝》、《曾子事父母》等。从这些篇目可以看出，对孔子孝道的弘扬，曾子贡献尤其巨大。同时，唐代柳宗元、宋代的程颐等人还认为《论语》是由曾子的弟子写成的。曾子是孔子晚年的学生，他对于孔子整体思想有较全面的领悟，因此，在答孔子问时，唯独曾子阐述了孔子思想中的"一贯"之道，与局限于谈论孔子礼乐观的学生明显不同。

子思以及思孟学派对孔子思想的继承与发扬。子思既是孔子的孙子，又是孔子的再传弟子。唐代学者韩愈认为子思的学问来自于曾子。汉代著名的历史学家司马迁认为子思创作了儒家的重要文献《中庸》，这一说法受到了后代人的怀疑，但尽管如此，《中庸》至少保存了子思的思想。《中庸》受到了后世儒者的高度重视，被认为是"孔门传授心法"，也就是传承孔子思想最为核心的著作。宋代的儒家学者更把《中庸》与《大学》、《论语》、《孟子》合为"四书"，成为儒家最主要的经典和理学的主要理论来源，对中国文化的发展产生了深刻的影响。

子思学说的重要性还在于作为儒学正统的孟子的学说受到了子思的启发，战国时期的思想家荀子就认为孟子是呼应子思的思想家。《孟子》中多次谈到曾子和子思。关于孔子—曾子—子思—孟子的正传系统，已受到后代学者的广泛认同。孟子是全面发展孔子思想的重要思想家，是继孔子之后秦代以前儒家的重要代表。他提出的性善论，完善了孔子的伦理思想。他

proposed, that is, the theory of basing government on humaneness, further developed Confucius' thought.

Then is about the changes made by Mr. Sun's school of Confucianism. A famous thinker of the Warring States was Xunzi; his name was Kuang, his style Qing. According to Han Fei, he was an outstanding representative of the Confucian school of Mr. Sun, and was a thinker as famous as Mencius. Xunzi absorbed Confucius' thought on humaneness-based ritual learning; he developed it into a comprehensive theory of rule by ritual, and provided a more comprehensive theoretical basis for practical government. The theory that Xunzi proposed about the evil of human nature, just like Mencius' theory on the goodness of human nature, in one aspect, developed Confucius' thought that "human natures are similar, and practice separates them." With regard to his view on the Way of Heaven, Xunzi is quite different from Mencius' view. Through his criticism of the intellectual thought of each school, Xunzi erected his own system of thought. His reception and transformation of Confucius' thought formed a new scenario in the development of Confucian learning.

Second is about the relation between Confucius and classical studies and occult learning. During the Warring States Period, Confucianism was just one school among the various schools. During the reign of Emperor Wu in the Han Dynasty, Confucianism came to enjoy a privileged position and became the orthodox brand of thought. The Han Dynasty saw the establishment of the official position of the academician that was based on teaching the Confucian classics, and classical studies hence flourished. This field itself split into two, "Modern Text Classical Studies" and "Ancient Text Classical Studies." "Modern Text Classical Studies" refers to classics collected and transmitted by Confucian scholars that were transcribed in the clerical script, the writing in common use at the time. Later scholars termed the study of these classics "Modern Text Classical Studies." "Ancient Text Classical Studies" refers to those Confucian classics written in the script of the Six States during the Warring States Period that had been discovered in the wall of Confucius' residence when Prince Gong of Lu demolished it; it also refers to those classics that circulated among the people and those stored in the imperial library that were written in ancient script. The classical scholarship devoted to these texts was called "Ancient Text Classical Studies." Classical scholarship on the modern texts emphasized elucidating the profound implications found in the "Six Classics," and was connected rather closely with the "apocryphal" texts that were popular during the Han Dynasty, which were colored by theology and superstition; they manifested a very strong theological flavor.

提出的仁政，也就是以仁为本的政治学说，发展了孔子的思想。

孙氏之儒对孔学的改造。战国时的著名思想家荀子，名况，字卿，是韩非所说的"孙氏之儒"的杰出代表，是与孟子齐名的思想家。荀子吸收了孔子以仁为本的礼学思想，发展成较全面的礼治理论，为现实政治提供了更为全面的理论依据。荀子提出的性恶论与孟子的性善论都从一个侧面发展了孔子的"性相近，习相远"的思想。在天道观方面，荀子与孔孟思想有较大的差异。荀子通过对各家各派学术思想的批判，建立起了自己的思想体系，他对孔子思想的继承与变异，形成了儒学发展的新局面。

二、孔子与经学、玄学。战国时期，儒学是百家之学中的一种，到了汉武帝时代，儒学受到独尊成为统治思想。汉代以儒家经典设博士官，经学盛行，其中又分为"今文经学"与"古文经学"。"今文经学"是指汉代的儒者搜集与传授儒家经籍，以当时通行的文字隶书记录下来，后人将他们的经学叫做"今文经学"；"古文经学"是指鲁恭王拆毁孔子住宅，在墙壁中发现了用战国时代六国文字书写的儒家经书，以及流传于民间和秘府中所藏的用古文写成的经书，以此为据的经学叫做"古文经学"。今文经学重在阐发《六经》中包含的深奥含义，与汉代流行的具有神学迷信色彩的"纬"书联系比较紧，表现

Classical scholarship on the ancient texts emphasized research in historical facts, thereby developing in the direction of elucidating ancient institutions and ancient script; they manifest a rather straightforward scholarly style. During the period between the end of the West Han Dynasty to the end of the East Han Dynasty, contentions broke out several times between the modern text school and the ancient text school. The main representative of the modern text school was Dong Zhongshu, who added the element of theology and formed a new system of Confucianism. This was a great change in the history of the development of Confucianism.

During the East Han Period, the study of "apocryphal texts" flourished. The *chen* part of the term "apocrypha" (*chenwei*) are texts that contain some superstitious prophecies; they utilize an esoteric form of language to provide mysterious explanations for the rise and fall of dynasties. The *wei* part of the term refers to texts that correspond to "classics" as they are elaborations of the meanings of the classics. They take as content the meaning of the Confucian classics, and add the fortunes and misfortunes, disasters and blessings of human affairs that prophesy the rise and fall of societies. The image of Confucius in the apocrypha is that of a spiritual prodigy who is able to foretell the future. Through the privileged position enjoyed by both the modern text school and the apocrypha during the Han Dynasty, the figure of Confucius became infused with a religious element. Of course, the changes made in Confucianism during the Han Dynasty by Dong Zhongshu and the study of the apocrypha were not incorporated within mainstream Confucianism of the later period. The transmission of ancient texts that avoided discussions of spiritual prodigies and adopted a simple form of textual exegesis was usually received by the majority of scholars, and gradually came to occupy the leading position in classical studies.

Apocryphal studies flourished during the periods of Wei, Jin, and South and North Dynasties. Hot topics of the time among scholars were questions that centered on whether or not "non-being" was able to spawn "being," and the relationship between being and non-being, and beginning and end; these debates formed occult learning. Although this was a cultural tide of thought characterized in the main by explaining and elaborating Daoist thought, nevertheless, these occultists also venerated Confucius, and honored him as a sage. For instance, the occultist Wang Bi regarded Confucius as "embodying non-being" and Laozi as embodying "being," since "non-being" was able to spawn "being" ; therefore, Confucius was more exalted than Laozi, and Confucius was a sage while Laozi was only a worthy. Of course, the Confucius

出深厚的神学色彩。古文经学重在考究史实，因而向阐述古代制度、古文字的方向发展，表现出比较朴实的学风。今文经学与古文经学在西汉末年到东汉末年经历了数次重要的争论。今文经学的主要代表是董仲舒，他将儒学宗教化，形成了一个儒学的新体系，在儒学演变历史上是一次大的变化。

东汉时期，"谶（chèn）纬"之学盛行，"谶"是一种迷信的预言，用隐语为朝代的兴亡提供神秘的理由。"纬"书是与"经"对称的对"经"书进行发挥的书。内容是以儒家经义，附会人事吉凶祸福，预言社会兴衰。纬书中的孔子成了可以预见未来的神灵。谶纬与今文经学一起在汉代通过儒学的独尊，而将孔子宗教化。当然，汉代董仲舒对儒学的改造以及谶纬之学并没有为其后的儒学主流所继承。不谈神怪、注释简明的古文经学往往为多数学者所接受，逐渐占据了经学的主导地位。

魏晋南北朝时期玄学盛行。当时的学者以"无"能不能生"有"为中心议题，讨论有与无、本与末的关系问题，形成了玄学。虽然这是以解释、发挥道家思想为主要特征的文化思潮，但是，玄学家们一般都很推崇孔子，尊孔子为圣人，如玄学家王弼就认为孔子"体无"，老子"体有"，"无"能生"有"，因此，孔子还是比老子高明，孔子为圣人，老子为贤人。当然，

conceptualized by the occultists was no longer the Confucius as originally understood; instead he had already been turned into an occultist and a Daoist. In the same manner, the Laozi who "embodied being" himself was no longer the Laozi as originally understood. Therefore, what the tide of occult thought manifested was a blend of Confucianism and Daoism.

When Buddhism spread into China, it presented a very real challenge to Confucianism. During the Southern and Northern Dynasties as well as Sui and Tang periods, Buddhism was particularly flourishing. A multifaceted theoretical conflict broke out between Buddhism and the culture of Confucianism. Although Buddhism broadly influenced society with its rather strong component of critical thinking, Confucianism still maintained its leading position in such fields as politics and education. At the same time, during the course of sinification, Buddhism manifested an active trend towards convergence with Confucian culture. All of this helped to prepare the way for the merging of Confucianism and Buddhism. After the mid-point of the Tang Dynasty, a group of critics with Han Yu being representative were dissatisfied with the unified situation of classical studies. They advocated returning to Confucius and Mencius, and based on their own subjective experience to grasp the "true spirit" of Confucius and Mencius. If they could directly seek Confucian thought from primitive sources, this would allow them to compete with Buddhism that was currently popular. This direction was continued by a large group of scholars during the beginning of the North Song Dynasty, and ultimately led to the creation of the rational study in Song period.

Third is about Confucius and rational learning. Rational learning (also known as Neo-Confucianism) during the Song, Yuan, and Ming periods, was the ruling thought during the later period of Chinese feudalistic society, and was reverenced as the philosophy of bureaucrats. The main canon of rational learning was the "Four Books" : the *Great Learning*, the *Doctrine of the Mean*, the *Analects*, and *Mencius* instead of the "Five Classics" (the *Book of Poetry*, the *Book of Documents*, the *Rites*, the *Book of Changes*, and the *Spring and Autumn Annals*), which had been venerated ever since the Han Dynasty. The *Analects,* the *Great Learning* and the *Doctrine of the Mean* that elucidated Confucius' thought as well as the work of Mencius, a transmitter of Confucian learning, were considered as the canon of rational learning. This obviously proves that Confucius' position had been elevated even further, demonstrating that Confucius was the founder of scholastic Confucianism. Of course, rational learning was also called "Neo-Confucianism," implying that there was something different in the Confucianism of the time from what

玄学家们所理解的孔子已不是原本意义的孔子，而是将孔子玄学化、道家化。同样，"体有"的老子也不是原本意义上的老子。因此，玄学思潮体现出的是儒家和道家融合的色彩。

佛教的传入使儒家文化受到了一次真正的挑战，南北朝时期和隋唐时期佛教尤其盛行，佛教与儒家文化产生了多方面的理论冲突，佛教以其思辨性较强的特征产生了广泛的社会影响。但尽管如此，儒学在政治、教育等方面仍然占据着主导地位。同时，佛教在中国化的过程中也表现出了与儒家文化主动趋同的姿态，这一切都为儒家与佛教融合提供了准备。唐代中期以后，以韩愈为代表的一批学者不满于唐代经学的统一局面，主张回到孔孟，以自己的主观体验，把握孔孟的"真正精神"，从儒学的原始文献中直接寻找儒学思想，以便与当时流行的佛教相对抗。这一取向被北宋前期的一大批学者所继承，并最终导致了宋代理学的产生。

三、孔子与理学。宋、元、明时期的理学（又称新儒学）是中国封建社会后期的统治思想，被奉为官方哲学。理学的主要经典依据是"四书"（《大学》、《中庸》、《论语》、《孟子》），而不是汉代以来尊奉的"五经"（《诗》、《书》、《礼》、《易》、《春秋》）。《论语》和阐发孔子思想的《大学》、《中庸》以及孔学传人孟子的著作被列为理学的经典，足以看出孔子的地位进一步得到了提高，说明了孔子才是儒学的开创者。当然，理学又被称为"新儒学"，意味着这时的儒学已与孔子所讲的儒学

Confucius had taught. One reason for this was that rational learning during the Song and Ming had not only inherited traditional Confucianism, at the same time it also absorbed the thought of Buddhism and Daoism; nevertheless, the core value system of Confucianism had not changed. Scholars of rational learning made a theoretical excavation of the thought of "the humane love others" in the *Analects* and developed it further, from which they created the very vital philosophy of human life that all living things in the world form a single entity. The Confucian classics thus revealed a theoretical theme that upto the present retains a very fresh, practical application, thus opening up a new realm in the development of Confucianism, and giving a new color to the image of Confucius. Simultaneously, rational learning scholars stressed the content of Confucian moral ethics. The moral vision of rational learning in Song and Ming periods was rather different from Confucius' theory of humaneness; this particular transformation in rational learning within Confucianism caused much severe criticism to be directed at Confucius in modern times.

Fourth is about the flux in reputation of Confucius and Confucianism in recent times. Through evidential research, scholars in the Qing Dynasty attempted to restore the original significance of Confucius' thought. Yet, since the start of the Opium War, China suffered from invasions by foreign nations, and the Chinese people faced unprecedented crises. It was precisely under these major circumstances that aggressive intellectuals displayed the banners of science and democracy at the beginning of the 20th century. They undertook a complete critique of traditional Chinese culture; as the representative of traditional culture, Confucius was the attention of the most severe attacks with the shouting of the slogan of "topple the Confucian shop!" Although Confucius truly harbored some backwardness and feudal elements, it is obviously unfair to blame all of the backwardness of Chinese science and technology during the recent past on cultural elements. The criticism leveled at Confucianism and Confucius himself was heavily influenced by the ideology resulting from the crisis facing the nation. In the main it was limited to the level of emotional and simplistic negation. Therefore, recent criticism of Confucianism and of Confucius has been unable to truly eliminate them. Nevertheless, a group of intellectuals has been able to dispassionately analyze the modern values inherent in traditional Confucianism.

Between 1966 to 1976, Confucius as well as Confucianism were again subjected to comprehensive criticism, but by the same token, it did not prevent a group of intellectuals from engaging in rational analysis. Especially

有所不同，原因之一是宋明理学既继承了儒学传统，同时又吸收了佛教和道家思想，但是，儒家的核心价值观念并没有改变。理学家们将《论语》中"仁者爱人"的思想进行了理论发掘与发展，从而形成了世间万物为一体的极富生态意义的生命哲学，从儒学经典中揭示出了至今仍具有鲜明现实意义的理论命题，开辟了儒学发展的新境界，为孔子的形象赋予了新的色彩。同时，理学家强化了儒学道德伦理的内涵，宋明理学的道德观念与孔子的仁学有较大的差异，理学对儒学的这一变异，使孔子在近代受到了严肃的批判。

四、近代以来孔子及儒学的兴衰起落。清代的学者们通过考据的方法努力恢复孔子思想的原初意义。而自从鸦片战争开始，中国遭受列强的入侵，中华民族遇到了空前的危机。正是在这样的大背景之下，激进的知识分子在20世纪初打出了科学与民主的旗号，对中国传统文化进行了全面的批判，作为中国传统文化代表的孔子便受到了猛烈攻击，他们喊出了"打倒孔家店"的口号。虽然儒学中确实存在着封建落后的成分，但是，将中国近代科学技术的落后完全归于文化因素，显然有失公允。这一时期对儒学以及孔子的批判受到强烈的民族危机意识的影响，主要限于情绪性的简单否定的层面，因此，近代对儒学与孔子的批判并没有能使儒学和孔学真正消亡，一批知识分子仍然能够冷静地分析传统儒学所具有的某些现代价值。

1966年至1976年，孔子以及儒学再一次受到了全面的批判，但这同样没有阻止一批知识分子对儒学进行理性分析，尤其是

given the grand background of diverse world culture, uncovering the modern value of Confucian culture has become a topic that has seized the attention of Western and Chinese scholars alike. In this regard, contemporary Neo-Confucians are making new efforts to formulate a third wave in Confucian studies. The first wave indicates the spread of Confucius' thought throughout the major feudal states until it became the national ideology, or official learning recognized by all during the West Han. The second renaissance was when Confucian studies gradually spread to Korea, Japan, and Southeast Asia. The third tide was when Confucian studies gradually became an important factor in the revolution of western philosophy, and shook up western philosophy. In the course of deeply penetrating these cultures, Confucianism itself became qualitatively enriched and reformed.

In 1978, after the reformation and opening up, and following the increasing apprehension of Western culture, the people's understanding of traditional Chinese culture went through a winding and tortuous course. Nevertheless, a renewed evaluation of Confucius as well as a deeper, more rational analysis of Confucian culture gradually took the lead. Confronting with the modern societies with Confucian components in East Asia and Southeast Asia and the realities of economic expansion, scholars have been rationally analyzing the internal values of Confucian culture. At the same time, Confucius and Confucian culture have been the object of broad-scale attention from the world. Following the rapid development of the Chinese society and economy, China has already become part of the international community that exerts an important influence on international politics and the world economy. Chinese culture is receiving more and more attention from the world, and as the most important representative of Chinese culture, Confucius has gained the universal veneration of the entire world.

在世界多元文化的大背景之下，发掘儒家文化的现代价值，成为中西学人共同关注的课题。在这方面，当代新儒家进行了新的努力，形成了儒学的第三次浪潮。此前的第一次浪潮是指孔子的思想传遍各主要诸侯国，直到西汉成为公认的国家意识形态（官学）。第二次中兴是儒家学说逐渐向朝鲜、日本以及东南亚传播。第三次浪潮就是儒学逐渐成为西方哲学革命的一个重要因素而产生的对西方哲学的冲击。儒学在深入渗透到其他文化的过程中，其本身也在质的意义上得到丰富和改造。

1978年改革开放以后，随着对西方文化的逐步了解，人们对中国传统文化的认识经历了曲折的过程，但是，对孔子的重新评价，对儒家文化进行深入理性的分析已逐渐占据上风，面对东亚、东南亚儒家文化圈现代社会、经济发展的现实，学者们理性地分析了儒家文化的内在价值。同时，孔子以及儒家文化也受到了世界的广泛重视。随着中国社会经济的快速发展，中国已成为国际政治、世界经济中具有重要影响的一部分，中国文化也越来越受到世界的广泛重视，而作为中华文化最重要代表的孔子也受到了全世界的普遍景仰。

Suggested Readings

Kuang Yaming.

Critical Biography of Confucius. Nanjing: Nanjing University Press, 1990.

Qian Mu.

Biography of Confucius. Shanghai: Sdxjoint Publishing Company, 2002.

Herbert Fingarette.

Confucius: The Secular as Sacred. New York: Harper Torchbooks, 1972.

Meng Peiyuan.

Meng Peiyuan's Lectures on Confucius. Beijing: Beijing University Press, 2005.

Hall, David and Roger T. Ames.

Thinking Through Confucius. New York: State University of New York Press, 1987.

Jin Jingfang, Lu Shaogang and Lu Wenyu.

New Biography of Confucius. Changchun: Changchun Press, 2006.

建议阅读书目

《孔子评传》，匡亚明著，南京大学出版社 1990 年版。

《孔子传》，钱穆著，三联书店 2002 年版。

《孔子：即凡而圣》，（美）赫伯特·芬格莱特著，江苏人民出版社 2002 年版。

《蒙培元讲孔子》，蒙培元著，北京大学出版社 2005 年版。

《通过孔子而思》，（美）郝大维、安乐哲著，北京大学出版社 2005 年版。

《孔子新传》，金景芳、吕绍纲、吕文郁著，长春出版社 2006 年版。

Translator's Notes

The short biographical study of Confucius contained in the concise edition of *Critical Biographies of Chinese Thinkers* is concise only in terms of length, not depth. For the author of the original biography of Confucius, Kuang Yaming, the distinguished general editor of the original series, had produced a masterful biographical tour de force. The concise version merely pared away most of the supporting edifice of the original: much historical background, cultural exposition, and institutional clarification, all discussion of sources and their validity, nearly all the supporting evidence, and all of the excurses on the lives of Confucius' contemporaries and disciples. But, happily for modern readers of the concise version, all of the main lines of thought and Kuang's authoritative conclusions made the transition still resonate and persuasive. Confucius is still revealed as a man of flesh and blood, of passions and aspirations, of triumphs and tragedies, and of surpassing cultural and intellectual import, all just had he been originally constituted by Kuang with great skill and empathy.

Equally impressive for readers is that the immediate impact of Kuang's vigorous prose still remains. Advanced students of Chinese will find much to challenge them linguistically just as Kuang's conclusions stimulate all readers intellectually. The editor of Kuang's original volume deserves kudos for this dual-accomplishment. To reduce the original with little loss of the core content, and to simultaneously reflect the vigor of the original stylistics are achievements that called on all the resources of an accomplished scholar and sensitive stylist. I congratulate just such a scholar and stylist.

As the English translator of this concise version, it was my pleasure during the course of my work both to be edified by the content while being stimulated by the literary sensibility and evocative imagery of the language. Either aspect makes the work worthy of careful and enjoyable perusal, but to have both is a rare treat indeed. I hope that the English version of this concise bilingual edition will be an adequate guide to the original thought; for the beauty of the language, however, readers will have to access it on whatever level possible for them individually. But whether advanced student or native speaker, both will be amply rewarded by the dual impact this little gem of a book makes on the minds and hearts of readers.

<div style="text-align: right">

Dr. David B. Honey
Mid-Autumn Festival, 2009
Wutaishan, Nanjing

</div>

图书在版编目(CIP)数据

孔子:汉英对照/周群著:(美)霍尼(Honey, D.)译.
—南京:南京大学出版社，2010.3(2012.6重印)
(中国思想家评传简明读本)
ISBN 978-7-305-06611-5

Ⅰ.孔…　Ⅱ.①周…②霍…　Ⅲ.孔丘(前551～前479)
—评传—汉、英　Ⅳ.B222.2

中国版本图书馆CIP数据核字(2009)第237553号

出 版 者　南京大学出版社
社　　址　南京汉口路22号　邮　编　210093
网　　址　http://www.NjupCo.com
出 版 人　左　健

丛 书 名　《中国思想家评传》简明读本(中英文版)
书　名　孔　子
著　者　周　群
译　者　David B.Honey
审　读　张　静
责任编辑　李海霞　　　　编辑热线　025-83685720

照　排　江苏凤凰制版印务中心
印　刷　江苏徐州新华印刷厂
开　本　787×1092　1/16　印张 12　字数 233千
版　次　2010年3月第1版　2012年6月第2次印刷
ISBN 978-7-305-06611-5
定　价　28.80元

发行热线　025-83594756
电子邮箱　Press@NjupCo.com
　　　　　Sales@NjupCo.com (市场部)